Passing Time

A Four Year Diary
1993 thru 1996

Anthony (Tony) Melli

iUniverse, Inc.
New York   Bloomington

Passing Time
A Four Year Diary 1993 thru 1996

iUniverse books may be ordered through booksellers or by contacting:

iUniverse
1663 Liberty Drive
Bloomington, IN 47403
www.iuniverse.com
1-800-Authors (1-800-288-4677)

Because of the dynamic nature of the Internet, any Web addresses or links contained in this book may have changed since publication and may no longer be valid.

ISBN: 978-1-4502-6358-0 (sc)
ISBN: 978-1-4502-6359-7 (dj)
ISBN: 978-1-4502-6360-3 (ebk)

Printed in the United States of America

iUniverse rev. date: 11/5/2010

Passing Time

A Four Year Diary
1993 – 94 – 95 – 96

Introduction

This introduction to my book,
I hope will make you further look,
To look inside my poems to read,
To see what life my mind did feed.

Some life events in which I engage,
I found a need to write on the page,
Those were the times I had an urge,
Upon the page my thoughts to purge.

Poems in this book I wrote for me,
And if you look within to see,
I think inside you well may find,
A memory lost brought back to mind.

Want you to know this introduction,
Not meant to be a sales seduction,
Your curiosity was meant to attract,
In hope with the book you'd interact.

But if this effort somehow does fail,
And with not to read you do prevail,
If time in this book you don't invest,
I still want to wish you the very best!

Tony Melli
06-12-2010

Empty Nest

Tonight my time I will invest,
To understand an empty nest,
My youngest soon will fly away,
The empty nest will come that day.

My wife and I that day will see,
The way our household used to be,
When youngest from the nest has flown,
My wife and I then – home alone.

The nest again will empty be,
The two of us – my wife and me,
Will be alone as once before,
No children in and out the door.

No son-in-law to pester us,
No messy cat to cause a fuss,
No daughter on the floor with phone,
My wife and I – are home alone.

The empty nest – though makes me sad,
The empty nest – is not all bad,
It gives me joy to know my wife,
Will share with me this nest for life.

But there's no power can take away,
My children in the nest will stay,
Within the nest – this heart in me,
My children will ---- forever be.

01-01-1993

Class

On New-Years day I raised a glass,
To toast with members of this class,
Since all of you could not be there,
I'll post this on the board to share.

To share with you for Ninety-three,
The warmth of friendship given me,
Friendships here within this class,
Were on my mind when raised this glass.

For all within this class my host,
And when I raised my glass to toast,
I raised it to my personal need,
It's friendship makes my life succeed.

So with term of Ninety-three begun,
I must confess to everyone,
On New-Years day I raised a glass,
To all of us --- within this class

01-02-1993

I flew the families I was Pilot for to Hot Springs, Arkansas for a
several day function.   I wrote the following while watching on
TV, Bill Clinton's, inaugural celebration.

Inauguration

I watch with mixed emotions -
try not to take it hard,
Assess my patriotic devotion –
to this changing of the guard.

Yes I make evaluation –
on this change of President,
And I watch with trepidation –
my inner thoughts to vent.

I look back on our history –
events in which I played,
And to me there is no mystery –
from moral path we've strayed.

The man we have elected –
the man now on display,
In the lifestyle he selected –
puts my thoughts in disarray.

As I watch the honors given –
to this new Commander-in-Chief,
I find my thoughts are driven –
and they offer no relief.

How a man who left his nation –
answered not its leaders call,
Now assumes Commander's station –
with no credence orders all.

I watch this pomp and circumstance –
presidential motorcade,
Shouting people, song and dance –
in his honor this parade.

While I alone within this room –
on this inaugural day,
Will put away my sense of doom –
and for the future pray.

To freedom's process add my voice –
and for the time will heed,
The office, not the man of choice –
the man who now does lead.

For I know the nations honor, keep –
come from ethics it is given,
And from this day we soon will reap –
by the morals he is driven.

So I'll give him what his office due –
then some future date reflect,
On what his actions did accrue ---
I pray honor and respect.

01-20-1993

While still there in Hot Springs, with time on my hands, I
let my mind wander and wrote the following thoughts to
relieve my concerns. It is self-explanatory.

Ross *Perot*

You supporters of Ross Perot –
I want you all to know –
You did your country ill –
When you exercised your will.

I'll make this statement brief –
We all may come to grief –
When with your support you sent –
Not the best to be President.

I watched with some dismay –
Nation's fabric stripped away –
For this man you helped elect –
By his actions commands no respect.

So I want you all to know –
You supporters of Ross Perot –
The votes that you gave to Ross –
Becomes the nation's loss.

And that loss may be oh so great –
And the time may be then too late –
When his flaws we all discover –
There may be no time to recover.

I hope I'll be proven wrong –
That he will be a President strong –
That his ethics he'll re-arrange –
And his basic character change.

But that chance I believe is small –
And someday we may recall –
That the nation received great blow –
And the culprit was --- Ross Perot.

01-22-1993

From Hot Springs we flew back home to Austin, Texas. Shortly
thereafter, I flew some of the families and two distinguished
guests to Acapulco, Mexico. The following few poems are a
reflection of my thoughts on some of the events that I felt the
need to express. I left the aircraft and passengers there and the
following day flew back commercially to Austin.
The first that follows was written in Acapulco

Acapulco Odyssey, I

On February First – in Nineteen-ninety-three,
I flew from Austin Texas – Old Mexico to see.
The trip had long been scheduled – from Monday to the next,
But somewhere in the journey - there came a change to text.

From Monterrey to Acapulco – was then that I first learn,
No longer on a Monday – but a Tuesday would return.
That change although seems minor – in Mexico you see,
At the whim of some officials – can harsh and painful be.

Then not the time to worry – there was a need to fly,
And mind must stay in focus – on duties in the sky.
For the sky is unforgiving – if you let attention stray,
You are looking for disaster – in events that come your way.

So the flight was uneventful – though wind was on the nose,
And flight path we were given – longer than the one I chose.
After landing Acapulco – and my journey friends depart,
With ground details completed – to the Radisson did start.

Now my thoughts do wander – to events that brought me here,
To this Bay of Acapulco – and the beauty that is near.
But this poem I cannot finish – for it's truly just begun,
It must wait until that Tuesday – when the Odyssey --- is done.

Pariso Radisson Hotel
02-01/02-1993

The next poem was begun in Austin and completed in Mexico. I
had a dear Doctor friend in our Sunday School Class at church
who was giving the lessons. He and I got into a discussion on
choice and resulting from that talk he told me the thrust of his
next lesson would be on freewill and choice. That gave me the
urge to write the following poem.

Doctrine

We soon will join together – some of us,
Our thoughts about freewill – to then discuss,
The concepts of our choice – we'll try to see,
If what we choose to do – from will that's free.

Thought process our – Creator did instill,
Not given from a choice – of our freewill,
As neither was this life – that we will lose,
A gift from our Creator – ours to choose.

There are philosophers – who do expound,
That teachings of freewill – is doctrine sound,
A concept saying – what in life we take,
Determined by freewill – free choice we make.

Determined leads to other – school of thought,
The concepts of – another doctrine taught,
Opponents of freewill – this teaching find,
Determinism doctrine – shapes the mind.

Determinism thence – we must explain,
For those who do not know – to make it plain,
Determinism's teachings – seek to show,
Pre-destination – opts – events we know.

Pre-destination – many do believe,
The Power of the All Knowing – did conceive,
To Mighty God – is nothing left un-shown,
From first creation – to the end is known.

So any act in life – we choose to do,
Not really from freewill – to me and you,
For all events – those past and yet to be,
All governed by the end – pre-destiny.

But either school of thought – we can refute,
For neither offers proof – that's absolute,
Philosophers – and theologians too,
Conjecture on unknowns – as me and you.

So with no facts between us – to discuss,
The choice, free choice – is left alone to us,
It matters not – which doctrine we will choose,
The life we know – with either one will lose.

Discussion then – is for the here and now,
To probe freewill – and what our thoughts allow,
Could there be choice – another doctrine found?
That blends the two – is there another ground?

We know that choices – by all must be made,
And with each choice – are all life's dramas played,
The end result – if choice or destiny,
Still comes by choice – though free it may not be.

So at the end – if freewill doctrine wrong,
That each choice made – was structured all along,
Should comfort bring – for then in truth can say,
There was no wrong – there only was one way.

My thoughts I know – are labored, convoluted,
But by my choice – within my mind were rooted,
Freewill or not – it matters not where blame,
Choices make of life – an interesting game.

A game where all – the players on the field,
Are tied to what - their faith and logic yield,
With life's events – they have no choice but deal,
Freewill ? – the end – that answer will reveal.

Or maybe not – the end may be the end,
There may be naught – beyond life to extend,
Life but a game – to see how well you played,
And with the end – your debt for playing paid.

After death – when life has been destroyed,
The mind may be – a black and empty void,
From every thought – from every sense may break,
No more, no more – are choices there to make.

But gamble not – on that scenario,
Life's too complex – another life does show,
Another side – beyond the veil a voice,
That says to all – you have, you have a choice.

A choice that goes – beyond this life on earth,
Each choice determines – what the soul is worth,
We could go on – in useless, long conjecture,
I choose not to – this ends my freewill lecture.

It ends for now – the thoughts my mind have travelled,
Thoughts put to rhyme – that here I have unraveled,
Was it my choice – this course of action take?
I leave to you – the choice that you will make.

Acapulco Day's Inn   02-06/07/08-1993

Acapulco Odyssey, II

With some anticipation – return I did Sunday,
To continue with the odyssey – to Acapulco Bay.
Yes with anticipation – for events that brought me here,
With break in communications – changed from plans so clear.

The date for our departure – one day had been delayed,
That one day could be most crucial – for on my planning played.
Not just the date of leaving – but who would come and go,
Till late within the planning – the final list did know.

Still more to my discomfort – in final days did learn,
In Mexico not staying – to Austin would return.
In these changes many pitfalls – for in Mexico the law,
Depends on who interprets – what in their statutes saw.

I tried to give good counsel – tried to make it plain,
What we faced in Acapulco – the potentials did explain.
After weighing valued input – for Old Mexico to see,
I felt a great commitment – on the trust was placed in me.

I put my cares behind me – to Mexico then flew,
And followed plan of action – that in Mexico renew.
I feel certain all will go well – back to Texas will return,
And for me will be a lesson – from this Odyssey to learn.

But must wait till back in Texas – for the Odyssey not done,
Till safe landing there in Austin – and the final poem begun.

02-08-1993   Acapulco Day's Inn

Acapulco

Last night in Acapulco – part of the night did share,
In Casa Tres Palabros – with friends residing there.
In a royal, cultured setting – with valued friends around,
The best of Acapulco – at Balcones de Luna found.

To the east of Acapulco – upon a cliff side high,
The view of bay and city – breathtaking to the eye.
The city lights, the harbor – the stars in sky so bright,
All blend to make that moment – a time of joy, delight.

The talk was light and casual – drink and food were fine,
Yes the night was like a mixture – of the finest, purest wine.
The time relaxed, passed quickly – with pleasantries depart,
And with my fellow traveler – back to hotel did start.

We left this regal setting – to world outside did go,
From the very best of living – to the other side we know.
Now I see in life the process – that allows both sides to be,
And I know it gives the balance – to renew life's energy.

Life is there for all to savor – and it's up to each to find,
The best of life abounding – to arrive at -- peace of mind.
It's the good and bad together – the rich, poor, everyone,
Who put the spice in living – that's been since time begun.

I evaluate life's happenings – All the things I hear and see,
And last night in Acapulco – was a slice of life -- -- to me.

Acapulco Day's Inn
02-09-1993

Acapulco, III

On Tuesday back to Austin –
return we did this day,
To finish with the saga –
of Acapulco Bay.

Despite the way it started –
first plan in disarray,
The final plans went smoothly –
and naught got in the way.

Our stay in Acapulco –
held much uncertainty,
Because our stay extended –
bordered on illegality.

For required regulations –
to be followed without flaw,
With the aircraft documentation –
on the fringe of Mexican law.

Yes there we were exceeding –
the time for us to go,
And with different people leaving –
that we didn't let them know.

So by need I treaded lightly –
a diplomat's role I played,
With Commandant and Immigrations –
enlisted professional aid.

It worked to great perfection –
relieved and pleased was I,
When we flew from Acapulco –
and we bid that place goodbye.

To McAllen then to Austin –
in a buoyant mood returned,
Now that safely back in Texas –
don't return is lesson learned.

Don't return unless you're willing –
to take risks in Mexico,
For is nothing there that certain –
if you can't, don't go, don't go.

Austin, Tx
02-09-1993

The following thoughts were during and following a Sunday
School discussion in which ego became, briefly, a side issue.

Ego

I put my ego on the shelf –
So I could look into myself –
And when I saw my inner track –
I quickly pulled my ego back.

For what I saw there deep inside –
I thought it best from you to hide –
Now that my ego's back in me –
I'll hide those things you should not see.

These words I did not seek to find –
But thoughts came quickly to my mind –
When in the class discussion strayed –
And ego, central theme now played.

It didn't seem to be quite right –
When ego put into bad light –
For ego is the binding glue –
That bonds reality to you.

When I put my ego on the shelf –
I am no longer then myself –
A different person now in there –
My psyche and self are off somewhere.

So I wrap my ego tight around me –
To hide those things you should not see –
I mask the bad and ugly too –
And expose my best façade to you.

That part of me you see and hear –
Is the covering of a thin veneer –
It's the part of me I want to show –
And I cloak the rest with my ego.

Thus ego becomes a necessity –
It gives my self-esteem to me –
It is to me more than a shield –
It's what I am -- -- it's me revealed.

02-15/16-1993

The next written on the ongoing political situation of the day.

Dear Ross

I hear with mixed emotions –
the things you have to say,
But I'll still join with others –
to send these bucks your way.

For again you are a salesman –
though I don't completely agree,
You've backed me into a corner –
to get support from me.

There was a time your actions –
earned you my respect,
I found you a man with values –
in those battles you select.

Then came the last election –
though I liked how you began,
You ended shrill and divisive –
came in poorly, an "also ran".

I send two poems I've written –
as well as support you've sought,
To show my mixed emotions –
in the dilemma of my thought.

Nation is caught in a nightmare –
if honor we expect to retrieve,
Then in United We Stand America –
I have to accept and believe.

03-02-1993

During a poetry session, I was fortunate to meet a wonderful
poet. This next reflects my feelings towards her.

Black/White

I find myself in Tyler –
in quiet reflective thought,
As I read the note you sent me –
with your poetry I am caught.

Those clippings you included –
review from Plain View Press,
Confirm what I know of you –
the good of you they stress.

The poem you wrote of Polly –
the depth of emotions shown,
Are reminders of life's trial –
the joys and sorrows known.

I am in a mood of your making –
in your note to me I find,
The pleasure poetry brings me –
the gentle persuasion of mind.

So I wanted now to tell you –
of my joy and my delight,
In a lady will live forever –
a great poet – Brenda Black White.

03-06-1993
Tyler, Tx

The following was written as I was waiting for a flight from Chicago's O'Hare airport to St. Louis. I was en-route to St. Louis from Austin, Texas for annual aircraft proficiency simulator training, and an FAA required check ride in a visual Flight simulator. The flight was diverted to Chicago due to inclement weather in St. Louis that prevented landing.

Journey to Forever

I join in this, this game of life –
with pilgrims on a journey,
Inside this airport terminal –
with the people now around me.

Here at O'Hare where I wait –
along with many others,
Men and women, girls and boys –
and babies with their mothers.

All came today to fill this space –
by needs of life were driven,
Into this airport waiting room –
to play the part they're given.

Most are fellow travelers –
who came this place to share,
That now await an airline flight –
to fly them off somewhere.

Others here to meet someone –
now play the waiting game,
For airline schedules gone awry –
and weather is to blame.

The press of people, some upset –
their plans by weather changed,
Give ticket agents verbal heat –
cause plans were rearranged.

I watch the varied people here –
I look into their faces,
I see a blend of many things –
each one my mind embraces.

There is a man of stature small –
his face reflects his worry,
Two huge bags to cause concern –
he races in a hurry.

A mother with a babe in arms –
and the baby loudly crying,
Has another baby on the floor –
her admonitions he defying.

So many different people here –
with little way of knowing,
Why they joined me in this place –
or where it is they're going.

But people here that I observe –
in this journey, this endeavor,
Have joined with me in this my life –
on my journey to --- forever.

03-13-1993
Chicago O'Hare terminal

What follows are miscellaneous thoughts I had a need to express.

Dreams

There was a poet most will know –
Whose name was Edgar Allen Poe,
This poem I will now devote,
To review a poem that he wrote.

I see him standing on a beach,
And to his poet's mind I reach,
To analyze what he found there,
Thoughts that he and I do share.

So many of his poems I like,
Into my very soul they strike,
The poems about his love Lenore,
The Raven Classic – "Never More".

With gift of rhyme he used so well,
His poems weave a magic spell,
Now he controls my mood and thought,
As in his magic spell I'm caught.

I see him there upon the beach,
Grains of sand within his reach,
He stands alone upon the shore,
Amid the surf's tormented roar.

I see him with the grains of sand,
Slowly creeping from his hand,
I sense the turmoil in his mind,
As truth to life he tries to find.

Within the poet's rhythmic score,
He asks if life is nothing more,
He asks if all we see or seem,
Is but a dream within a dream.

The grains of sand within his grasp,
He could not save with firmer clasp,
They were reminders of the strife,
That this great poet found in life.

The falling sand he did compare,
With life's confusion everywhere,
But grains of sand not his to save,
With laws of nature must behave.

Now his poem – melancholy, sad,
Expressive of the thoughts he had,
In lighter mood with other thought,
Another poem might have brought.
If all in life we see or seem,
Is but a dream within a dream,
In my dream, in mood that's light,
A poem within a poem I'll write.

Life and dreams are intertwined,
By unknown forces were designed,
There is no great disparity,
They both are one and same to me.

Yes life and dreams sum total make,
And from them both my senses take,
The perceptions of a Master scheme,
In dream is life, in life is dream.

The grains of sand Poe tried to save,
From mercies of the pitiless wave,
Were responding to what had to be,
Resist his grasp and were set free.

They were not meant to be held tight,
For nature's forces, nature's might,
With grains of sand they do relate,
To guide them to their natural state.

The grains of sand returned to deep,
Back to the wave for beach to keep,
Released they were to nature's fold,
Back for the hands of time to hold.

The hands of time and nature's force,
Keep all things on a steady course,
There is no need to weep or cry,
If my desires they defy.

If dream within a dream is true,
Then there is nothing I can do,
But do the best with dream I'm in,
Until the next dream I begin.

With help of Poe I've come to see,
The dreams and life in poetry,
That dreams and life as one begun,
And without either --- both are done.

03-22/23-1993
Gulfport, Ms

Change

I find myself in harmony,
With those events surrounding me,
Because my life in balanced state,
I find it easy to relate.

With things in balance, no surprise,
My life an easy exercise,
The course of things just flow my way,
Decisions easy ---- child's play.

Since everything for now in place,
There are no dilemmas here to face,
The present and the future too,
Not threatened by the things I do.

Would it that life were always so,
In unison with what I know,
Not perfect, but at least in hand,
With concepts that I understand.

But I know that's not reality,
I know that this can't always be,
I know all things not meant to last,
I know by looking at my past.

In an ever changing world I'm caught,
And by my past have I been taught,
That the future never is quite clear,
In this ever changing atmosphere.

So from the past I try to learn,
The bad and good from it discern,
The force of change is understood,
I try to change my life for good.

I've strayed from where this poem began,
When harmony through my mind ran,
Within my mind I wanted to draw,
The unity to life I saw.

But harmony by change replaced,
For all in life by change embraced,
With no change life could not grow,
There must be change full life to know.

The truth of change not overstated,
Time by change is liberated,
Change is to time a necessity,
Bears more than fruit of memory.

Without change all time would cease,
Abruptly stop, could not increase,
For change alone gives depth to time,
As changing words give depth to rhyme.

Thus change a vital part of me,
It sets my mind and Spirit free,
It helped my thoughts to rearrange,
From harmony --- to thoughts of change.

04-02-1993
Hot Springs, Ark

Who I Am

At times I think God just in mind,
That God is only there to find,
There is no God to man relation,
That God is my imagination.

But other times with what I know,
To other thoughts of God I go,
That God fulfills my greatest need,
Without which I cannot succeed.

I need a God to make me whole,
That's why there's God within my soul,
With God in me life will not end,
For God gives hope life to extend.

Yes God essential part of me,
I want God here for all to see,
I want the Power, I want the thought,
That everything by God is wrought.

For without God is nothing there,
There just is me to go nowhere,
Yes without God with logic know,
Back to oblivion mind would go.

Back to a bleak and empty place,
No thoughts for mind now to embrace,
As if my life had never been,
No present, future to live in.

I want much more than that to be,
And only God gives hope to me,
So I will do the best I can,
To try to meet a Godly plan.

If there's an after-life to lose,
It's up to me, to me to choose,
It's up to me now to decide,
What rules in life now to abide.

Yes only me – I'm in control,
Although at times God I extol,
It may be God who did Create,
But it is I who must relate.

I'm just not sure if God is there,
Or if of me God is aware,
It matters not – I'm still the same,
And I alone will bear the blame.

It is not easy must confess,
When faith in God I don't profess,
If there is a God – God really there,
Of my weak faith will be aware.

Yes all of this is understood,
That God will know my faith not good,
And when comes time for God's judgment,
God will decide where I'll be sent.

Thus I accept the role I'm in,
Try to determine what is sin,
In this my life of give and take,
My inner peace I try to make.

So when I come to that last door,
It will be me who set the score,
It will be me now to retell,
If I have earned a heaven --- hell.

It's then too late when I come to,
That final door must enter through,
Too late to change what must relate,
There no more time – then is too late.

If there is a God – God will understand,
God was the Maker – was God's hand,
Created all --- that did unfold,
And not my choice – to fill the mold.

For by God's thinking I designed,
And by God's hand was I aligned,
It was God who shaped the mold,
And this my mind for thoughts to hold.

God Creates --- but it is I,
Who makes the choices to live by,
It is up to me to know the wrong,
And make the choice where to belong.

There is a God and I rejoice,
That to believe becomes my choice,
Were there no God and God a sham,
I would not be the man I am.

No I would be just form and mold,
For just the hands of time to hold,
To live a moment on this earth,
And after that to lose my worth.

I am much more than what I seem,
Much more than fantasy or dream,
And all because it's clear to me,
That without God I wouldn't be.

With all I've said I am amused,
I find my thoughts of God confused,
I want a God to give relief,
A God who favors my belief.

And my belief I think is shown,
It is uncertain, it is unknown,
It is belief, if God is there,
That if I sin, my sin will share.

I think that God will share the blame,
Because from God, from God I came,
That God is Great and heavenly,
And God will share and care for me.

As you can see with God allied,
Although I see the other side,
In my confusion I will give,
Honor to God for life I live.

And I will try to meet the test,
To try to do my very best,
And after life with where I go,
The who I am --- at last will know.

04-03-1993
Majestic Hotel - Hot Springs, Ark.

The following thoughts were written after spending several
hours at St. Joseph's Hospital there in Hot Springs with close
and dear 96 year young friend, Mary Quinn. She had fallen and
had a severe gash on the back of her head that required stitches.
She was very independent, good humored, cantankerous, and
loving all at the same time. She liked living at the Majestic and
felt threatened with her age. Though she was 96, she was still
very active. With memory problems that go with old age, she
unfortunately was not very hygienic and having a pet cat did not
help the circumstances. She was smart but unaware of the
problems she was causing herself and the hotel. I had known
Mary many, many years and didn't know how to get through to
her. I did give to her what here is written.

Because I love you

It's because I love you Mary Quinn –
I now express my thoughts within –
And I know that I cannot delay –
After many hours we shared today.

What I'm about to write to you –
Is really hard for me to do –
I'm not quite sure just how to start –
But Mary dear it's from the heart.

I've watched you close and from afar –
So I know how independent you are –
I know how headstrong you can be –
With the feistiness in you I see.

As I watched you struggle to recall –
When it was you hurt your head in fall –
It was then I knew I must proceed –
To tell you of the help you need.

I know that you won't want to hear –
What has become so very clear –
I know by you will be denied –
That you need someone by your side.

And Mary not that your inept –
But Mary please try to accept –
What those in friendship try to give –
The help you need your life to live.

Oh Mary listen, continue to be –
A source of joy not pain to me –
I wish there were a better way –
These words within my heart to say.

Accept the friendships offered you –
Let those who care assist you do –
Those things in life because of age –
Require help now to engage.

Let them your hair and body groom –
And with your cat to clean your room –
It's now dear lady you must begin –
To let your friends – the sunshine in.

As must, the time for talking done –
With love this poem was begun –
Please understand what I've tried to say –
And Mary please --- do it now --- today.

04-09-1993
Majestic Hotel/Hot Springs, Ark

The following thoughts were transcribed into a micro-cassette
tape recorder and then transposed on paper after returning to
the Majestic Hotel in Hot Springs.

Pilot Time

To Little Rock – I drive this night,
To meet an inbound Southwest flight,
About nine-ten it will arrive,
Then back to Hot Springs I will drive.

And I will have at my right side,
Co-captain Roy to share the ride,
From Dallas Love he now does fly,
To crew a Merlin in the sky.

Tomorrow we'll crew a Turbo Prop,
With Glad Oaks Texas our first stop,
To an Easter party there to go,
And Roy will protest – this I know.

Parties are really not his thing,
He'd rather be in flight on wing,
Flying is what will get us there,
Se he will go and grin and bear.

He's a gentleman, he is well bred,
Though he'd rather be in flight instead,
He'll wait till party's said and done,
And the flight to Austin then begun.

Yes he's coming here with me to fly,
To crew our Merlin in the sky,
Except for urge to join in flight,
He'd rather not come here tonight.

Well in Little Rock at Adam's Field,
With journey done my mind must yield,
Must put an end to this aimless rhyme,
And like Roy look forward to – Pilot Time.

04-10-1993

This next was part of the classification presentation I was
required to give to the Rotary Club I was a new member of. It
began with a brief autobiography along with the poem.

Rotary

To the University Area Rotary –
Classification task asked of me –
To speak of my work history –
I will now recite through poetry.

As I begin – I cannot deny –
I've a fascination with the sky –
So at age seventeen I began to fly –
And now a Commercial Pilot am I.

When 29 years in the Air Force was done –
I continued flying just for fun –
And as that course of flying run –
Another career in aviation begun.

I find within my classification –
A mix of work and recreation –
The paper-work has its frustration –
But the flying brings a high sensation.

I'm the manager of a company –
That provides air travel for a fee –
A Swearingen Jet-Prop, Merlin Three –
With the Commercial Pilot being me.

As the manager I must relate –
$750.00 an hour the normal rate –
But that cost we can negotiate –
If your flying need is out of state.

As the Commercial Pilot I'll proceed –
To the general info you may need –
If you have an interest please take heed –
To the passenger data and aircraft speed.

Nine passengers in comfort can go –
270 miles in an hour to show –
That's the general data you need know –
So no other info your way will throw.

Well I've offered you my work relation –
To try to explain my classification –
As I join with you in this avocation –
I thank you for your confirmation.

But I pursue another classification –
An un-paid quest of my creation –
I record events affecting me –
As an observer of life through poetry.

Since a captive audience in you I hold –
For a few more minutes I'll be bold –
And use up my remaining time –
To abuse you with my attempt at rhyme.

05-06-1993

This next was a poem I had written to tender my resignation to the Rotary Club I was a member of. The attendance rules for Rotary were changed prior to my submitting that so since it was no longer applicable, I did not follow through.

Resignation

To the University Area Rotary –
The honor you bestowed on me –
To join your august company –
Has left me in a quandary.

Within the words I now state –
I hope my thoughts to you relate –
Rules I studied much too late –
For me some problems did create.

Since I agreed to join you all –
The fault alone on me does fall –
Was honored when you did install –
Me to join your Rotary call.

With dedication fresh and new –
I felt a bond with things you do –
But in the days that did ensue –
I find I have to part from you.

I'll try my best to now explain –
With priorities that I maintain –
Attendance rule cannot sustain –
So membership I can't retain.

In careful thought did I begin –
Troubled words you find within –
I find with rules I cannot win –
Return to you your tape and pin.

I use this rhythmic incantation –
To tender you my resignation –
It comes not with protestation –
I feel we've had a good relation.

This resignation to you sent –
Is from the heart with good intent –
Again --- is not from discontent –
But meant to offer my lament.

Please accept what has to be –
It is what the rules demand of me –
Enjoyed your warmth and company –
And wish the best to --Rotary.

08-04-1993

Clan

Oh my name is Tony Melli –
I'm the father of this clan,
The lady who's the mother –
is my lover Myrtle Anne.

In the years we've been together –
our three daughters did evolve,
Three beauties who are married –
and three husbands now involve.

With their husbands clan expanded –
grandchildren did arrive,
This process of expansion –
is what makes the clan survive.

Oh the years go by as my life goes on –
to meet uncertain plan,
But I find myself in harmony –
as the father of this clan.

08-11-1993

Our Sunday School Faith Class had a member of mystery that
was always doing something special for another member of the
class. We never knew who that person was until his wife told as
some time after his death.

Phantom

Oh hail to the Faith Class Phantom –
that legend of mystery,
Hail to the Faith Class Phantom –
whoever that person might be.

Yes hail the Faith Class Phantom –
that person of thoughtfulness,
Who greets with words of affection –
the day of our birth to bless.

Oh hail to this giver among us –
who role of a phantom does play,
By keeping their person a secret –
as offer goodwill of the day.

Phantom seeks no attention –
using mystery to make us aware,
A miracle wrought on your birthday –
a paradox of life to share.

To remind that somewhere is someone –
composer has us in mind,
Created the day of our coming –
and ties to each other did bind.

Hail the Faith Class Phantom –
may phantom with us ever stay,
May phantom accept our blessings –
not on one, but on every day.

08-22-1993

This, that follows, was a Post Script to the previous poem.

To each member of the class I see –
You are more than but a phantom to me –
For I know that you contain much more –
Than I see standing there before.

There is no way for me to know –
With the outward signs to me you show –
The depth of all you have inside –
I know like me some things you hide.

The thoughts in you that I invest –
Is to credit you with the very best –
To give what friendship did accrue –
The respect and honor that you're due.

I've come to the bottom of the page –
So from this verse will disengage –
But I am sure this poem clearly shows –
That the phantom this poem did not compose.

This next was written with thoughts from a Faith Class lesson.

Commandments

When Moses came down from the mountain –
with the tablets made of stone,
There carved on the face of the tablets –
were words from God to be shown.

Carved in stone were the Ten Commandments –
that God to Moses did give,
And there bound within the Commandments –
God's Edict of how we should live.

Rules to be followed not broken –
God's Commandments to me and to you,
Rules that are clear and with meaning –
most specific sound easy to do.

If the Bible is book that you live by –
and your crosses in life are endured,
If you're faithful to law of Commandments –
then heaven for you is assured.

But we all break the Ten Commandments –
or the meaning within them that lie,
And there is the crux of the problem –
who interprets the code we live by.

For we're none of us, none of us perfect –
in dilemmas of life so intense,
It's their meaning that causes the problems –
as we try to use common sense.

So we study once more the Commandments –
as we listen to some other thought,
Knowing well that there isn't an answer –
as in arms of discussion we're caught.

Common sense is in the eye of the beholder –
and the Bible had this well in mind,
When it offered to us the Commandments –
as a means our salvation to find.

08-25-1993

Late one morning while on the couch, I fell fast asleep. I didn't sleep but about 15 minutes when something woke me. Although awake, I was still feeling the glow from a wonderful dream I was in the middle of. I quickly tried, but failed, to reconstruct emotion the dream had triggered. I wrote the following to try to help the process.

Love Sonnet

From depth of sleep – I awake from dream of you,
A pleasant dream – where life was fresh and new,
How sweet the dream – as scenes from out the past,
Caress my mind – with thoughts of you that last.

I try to write – the dream to rhythmic score,
The mystic spell – of dream somehow restore,
Too quickly though – the dream my mind forsakes,
Back to the day – my thoughts from sleep awake.

But while the aura – of dream of you still clings,
I'll savor this – the warmth of love it brings.

To my wife.

08-27-1993

This next poem I wrote on a conversation I had with a friend of mine concerning success in life. He was in a down mood.

Success

I doubt a person ever could –
    put value on their success,
To know which actions in the past –
    were the best for happiness.

I doubt a person ever was –
could measure their life well,
Could in this venture known as life –
the good or bad foretell.

Could know the road they travelled –
as the clock of life was run,
What part of all their actions –
caused battles lost or won.

We have to take each moment –
and put it into place,
For it balances with others –
the whole of life to trace.

That life is all these moments –
that to last moment lead,
And as we live in this moment –
we know fate may intercede.

Yes fate, that unplanned factor –
a strange and elusive force,
That takes control of a moment –
to put life on a different course.

Fate makes life uncertain adventure –
as we try success to attain,
But not till that final moment –
will we know if success we obtain.

Only when all moments are final –
when fate intervenes no more,
Free from all earthly endeavors –
only then can we total the score.

Use the moment to best advantage –
propels us leads to the last,
Moment is key to the future –
more crucial to moments of past.

The moments of past unchanging –
part of our life said and done,
This moment and those that follow –
determine success if it's won.

Success shows measure of living –
as poem with measured time,
Come with blending of moments –
poem with blending of rhyme.

Rhyme blends to have purpose –
flows with expression of thought,
Give this moment full meaning –
in rhythm of life will be caught.

Success is a hard thing to measure –
in moments of joy and stress,
But rhythm of life gives balance –
salvation that measures success.

09-04/05-1993
Boulder, Co/Saratoga, Wy

This next poem was a follow on in thought to the previous.

Dear Millie

When I wrote the poem success –
you and John were on my mind,
Following thoughtful conversation –
the meaning of success to find.

With a dear friend in Colorado –
a man I highly respect,
We spoke of our years together –
from memories that we select.

Spoke of the past with nostalgia –
memories of good times we had,
But then when we got to the present –
my friend seemed a little sad.

He felt that he wasn't achieving –
the goals in life he had set,
And now during our conversation –
he related to me his regret.

He related to me his discomfort –
with things he had left undone,
And to him it was a great burden –
success as he thought it not won.

I was surprised by his conversation –
for successful he was to me,
A man of great honor and stature –
much loved by his family.

I lectured that he should be thankful –
for blessings in life we received,
For the goals we know we completed –
successes we know we achieved.

He agreed as we counted our blessings –
in friendship shared that night,
Then I left to return to my lodging –
my thoughts in a poem to write.

But I had to use great concentration –
mind on success would not stay,
It wandered to friends that I treasure –
to you and to John it would stray.

It would stray to our Sundays together –
the good from you both I receive,
And trials you both were then facing –
as we searched for a faith to believe.

Like John I have faith in a Creator –
a God who together we shared,
A God though we questioned the motive –
a God who for all people cared.

I loved John his soft gentle nature –
a lift to my Spirit would give.
And the quiet reserve of his person –
in core of my memory will live.

I write this to honor John Douglas –
my emotions inside to reveal,
To express to the woman he married –
the joys and the sorrow I feel.

The joys I receive from your being –
the sorrow that John now away,
Puts me closer to God my Creator –
salvation for all now to pray.

I know that with God John is joking –
telling God what he would have done,
And God in God's wisdom does listen –
as relation in heaven begun.

Success for John not in question –
in high standard of living he met,
His attitude towards life an example –
of the principled goals that he set.

It pains me I missed his last service –
but in Spirit and mind I was there,
And I write this to ease my frustration –
I write this to tell you I care.

So Millie accept this weak offering –
this poem I write to express,
John to me was a man for all seasons –
who now rests in the arms of success.

09-10/11-1993
Austin, Tx/McAlester, Ok

A re-write of Amazing Grace follows.

Amazing Grace (Two)

Amazing Grace is balm to me –
the music fills my soul,
From pain of sin it sets me free –
it makes my Spirit whole.

A sacred calm comes over me –
no longer life to fear,
I sense a peace that's yet to be –
when sound of hymn I hear.

Tis not the words that comfort me –
though words they may apply,
But sound of hymn God's symphony –
brings awe I can't deny.

How sweet the joy that comes to me –
when God with hymn does share,
That He in me no wretch doth see –
and that for me does care.

Amazing Grace overpowers me –
the future now to face,
I feel the love, tranquility –
through God's Amazing Grace.

09-22-1993

Susan

Your All Saints Church awakes in me –
A special insight there to see,
My senses now - to me reveal –
Some deep emotions that I feel.

My senses to – this world now wake –
As from the past – my mind does break,
I feel my Spirit – open wide –
To a God that I – had once denied.

Oh life – oh vibrancy – of this day –
The pain of doubt – is washed away,
The depth of life's – reality –
In all its splendor – shown to me.

Life is not meant – in past to live –
This day – today – to me does give,
The reality of – the here and now –
Without the doubt – of why and how.

With all the good – surrounding me –
I have no doubts – why life must be,
My doubts have all – been answered by –
My God, the God – I once deny.

I know that life – will always exist –
And today helps me – my doubts resist,
My doubts with things – not understood –
Today no doubts – just peace and good.

Today my Spirit – by All Saints is driven –
By Creative design – new joy is given,
Today inner Spirit – gives me a choice –
To accept the good – and in life rejoice.

Again I find peace – inner Spirit commanding –
A peace that defies – all of my understanding,
At peace with God's Grace – in a Spiritual way –
I surrender myself – to the good – of today.

09-22-1993

This next is a copy of what I had sent via FAX to Elizabeth
Carpenter. The contents of the FAX was a poem I had just
written followed by a note explaining the poem.

Note: Carol Channing is in Austin to give a performance and,
I'm sure, to visit friends. I flew her once back in June of 1982 to
and from the LBJ Ranch to visit Mrs. Johnson. She was hosted
by Liz Carpenter who was with her friend, Mrs. Elizabeth
Talmadge. During the short flight from Austin to the ranch,
Carol came up front and sang me a song that only she can do
justice to. "Hello Captain Melli, well Hello Tony, it's so nice to
see you there where you belong, --- etc". Yes, I was surprised.

To the music of Hello Dolly

Carol

Hello Carol – well hello Carol –
It's so nice to see you back with friends you know,
You're looking swell Carol – I can tell Carol –
That in Austin you're a lady who will steal the show.

I flew you once Carol – with your hosts Carol –
To a ranch to visit Mrs. LBJ,
While up in flight Carol – you were gracious Carol –
When you sang to me you really, really made my day.

As your pilot Carol – you were great Carol –
At my shoulder you created for me a special song,
You sang it well Carol – you told me Carol –
You were glad that I was in the seat where I belong.

Well you were right Carol – but you know Carol –
That moment was the best of flights for me,
So cheers Carol – lots and lots and lots of love Carol –
Carol you are the very best – no one will ever take your place –
You're the classiest act the world will ever, ever see!!!!

10-05-1993

What is next, came from miscellaneous and extraneous thoughts
of the moment with the need to express.

Time

Time gives the harmony to living –
Each second, each minute and hour,
Measure passage in life unforgiving –
That substance of birth does devour.

Time travels in but one direction –
Always forward to never turn back,
From the onslaught of time no protection –
It is constant and on the attack.

Time is mystic, no matter or substance –
No physical properties to mold,
So you can offer no force or resistance –
To either hasten or strangle its hold.

To all things, to all things, consuming –
Signifies their beginning and end,
It is essential to life, most illuming –
As a mentor, an enemy, or friend.

Time, endless time, though a mystery –
By its evidence alone I am taught,
The goodness of life that surrounds me –
Only passage of time could have wrought.

Time, with no beginning or ending –
The leveler of all of mankind,
Is creation of God, God extending –
The mightiest of power --- God's mind.

10-21-1993

More miscellaneous, extraneous thoughts in Gulfport, Ms.
where I flew Engineers and Architects to a project they were on.

Design

Events in life around me –
are all in constant change,
The substance of creation –
time's process rearrange.

Forever forward going –
in transition all things grow,
To reach their full potential –
design of change must know.

This universe, this planet –
these mountains, rivers, seas,
All designed through evolution –
the stream of time to please.

Here in Gulfport Mississippi –
I joined with friends in talk,
By design we shared together –
this pathway in life we walk.

In respite from work's endeavor –
Engineer and Architect,
Dined and offered discourse –
on the subjects they select.

I enjoyed this kindred caucus –
the rapport with humor light,
And I reveled in the goodness –
that was offered me tonight.

Made me thankful of the process –
how in life the joy I find,
Is design gives life its meaning –
constant change to nourish mind.

10-28-1993
Gulfport, Ms., Best Western Seaway Inn

This next correspondence I submitted to the University Area
Rotary Club of Austin, of which I was a member. I feel sure the
identities mentioned will not object to my doing so, for I believe
the nature and content of the correspondence is very positive
and complimentary. I would not include if I thought otherwise.

General procedures have been followed since Jerry Galbraith
and I discussed to sponsor Millie Douglas for membership. With
my un-scheduled absences, that has been accomplished
primarily via verbal communications. Jerry and David Tobey
have assured me that the nomination is basically on track.
Membership application is submitted with this correspondence.
I hope this hasn't caused any problems.

Propose

Mildred Douglas whom many of you know –
as new member to the club we propose,
After all of her credentials we show –
We think none her membership will oppose.

I will begin with her classification –
to explain it I know we have need,
She trades in the field of education –
Adult Specialist the calling she heed.

With a B.A. & B.S. from Northwestern –
and her Masters here at U.T.,
She continued her Post Graduate Intern –
in the field of Counseling Psychology.

Yes Millie has all of the essentials –
to be accepted in Rotary,
She's a person with honored credentials –
and a good friend --- to Jerry and me.

I know you will all use good judgment –
welcome Millie to Rotary's fold,
And to let her join in our commitment –
the traditions of Rotary to uphold.

11-10-1993

This next is fairly self explanatory. It came from thoughts
following my 63rd birthday celebration given by my wife and
children and grandchildren.

Gifts

To Lisa, Mary and Myrtle –
For my beautiful daughters three,
I write this little missive –
On the gifts were given to me.

The socks and clock from Lisa –
Are in good use today,
While the socks and tie from Mary –
In her words, "What can I say".

Now the shirt received from Myrtle –
I like and wear a lot,
So I'll try to express in this poem –
Delight from the gifts that I got.

The gifts gave to me a good feeling –
For in them all I could see,
The source of my greatest treasure –
The love of my children for me.

Warm green shirt from the Griffiths –
From Watsons' the clock with a voice,
Contrast with the gifts from the Bullins –
In a silly mood – Mary's choice.

But Looney Tunes socks with Bugs Bunny –
Clock that tells me the time,
The cotton shirt sent from Seattle –
Not the reason for this rhyme.

It's joy I receive from my family –
The thrust of this poem did start,
It touched on my sixty-third birthday –
The sensitive chords of my heart.

11-15-1993
Dad/Granpa/Tony

This next is another of my miscellaneous thoughts to Rotary.

Believe

You "Believe in what you do" – with that sentence I begin,
My support – my pledge to you – to "Do what you believe in".
In first meeting as your guest – in depth of our discussions,
No conservative, liberal test – to free thought no repercussions.

Your fellowship I wholly embrace – you have qualities I admire,
You are all with social grace – and the intellect I desire,
Yes this University Club to me – in worthy deeds not lacking,
It is easy for me to see – you earn my respect and backing.

I will keep my pledge to you – for in Rotary I am certain,
You "Believe in what you do" – and "Do what you believe in".

11-19-1993

More miscellaneous thoughts generated by my Grandchildren.

Wonderland

Will you come with me to a wonderland –
That little children know,
Where Barbie Dolls and Choo Choo trains –
Peter Pan, Cinderella go.

Story book land with ice cream and cake –
Balloons and a million toys,
A fairyland place where treasures abound –
To please little girls and boys.

I watched grandchildren at their play –
I watched them as they relate,
To a fantasy place only they could design –
The vision that they create.

I could not interfere in their wonderland –
World they imagined in play,
For here the children are master of all –
I knew I would be in the way.

Yes wonderland is for children alone –
Grandfathers must not wander in,
It takes the innocent mind of a child –
For magic of play to begin.

But come with me to our wonderland –
Let us try to regain once more,
The magic of life as children in play –
The miracle of living restore.

11-22-1993

This next once again came from thoughts generated by the
Sunday School Faith Class my wife and I attended.

Spirit

There is a Spirit in our Class –
It seems nobody knows,
A Spirit with a touch of class –
Whose reputation grows.

This Spirit from the Phantom came –
Enforcing Phantom history,
Since Spirit, Phantom are the same –
Continues on the mystery.

We're pretty sure it's one of us –
Some think it may be Wanda,
While others say it's Andrew, Gus –
Fellows we are fonda.

There's Bev and Jimmie and Dorine –
Who have the great potential,
To offer gifts that we have seen –
These gifts of "self" essential.

But all within the class are dear –
From each I get great pleasure,
When they're around a Phantom's near –
For each is a Spirit treasure.

Treasure of goodness in them abides –
A bounty of giving and sharing,
Soul of a Spirit in each of them hides –
To offer much love and caring.

So here's to the Spirit, Millie or Dan –
Ray, or Jean our Class Poet,
Whoever the mystery, woman or man –
You're an angel and I want you to know it!!

12-11-1993

More miscellaneous thoughts with need to express.

Vision

From the nothing of darkness – the blackness of night,
Came the vision of morning – Creation ---- came light.
Came the vision of matter – came a vision exact,
It was vision of life – that with light could react.

From God came the vision – life properties to find,
Then from nothing created – the miracle of mind.
Light from the darkness – mind to perceive,
With no God there no vision – YES --- in God I believe.

Merry Christmas !!!!!!!!

12-24/25-93

This next was sent to local newspaper's Letters to the Editor.

I am responding to the letter to the editor published in your paper. My thoughts in the attached poem are to rebut the assertions of faith and belief there expressed in the column. Atheism, much like religiosity, requires a strong desire to believe, regardless of the fact that all evidence is in opposition to the belief. That being the case, I opt toward the thoughts I express in my poem, Common Sense. I don't expect this to be published, but as I have done in the past, I thank you for providing the means to vent my frustration.

Common Sense

Within this poem I'll dispense –
Thought process I call common sense,
I know that questioned I may be –
By those who with me disagree.

But with clear logic I will start –
Some common sense to now impart,
I begin with something can't deny –
That all who live will someday die.

Now this one fact is absolute –
That no clear thinker can refute,
For death the leveler of mankind –
So here a common ground we find.

Since common ground now sets the stage –
With common sense we can engage,
With common sense we can explore,
The logic of Creations core.

With common sense investigate –
The mystery of what does create,
With God or chance do we traverse –
This endless space – this Universe.

By ethereal power was all this wrought –
Undeniable force from Godly thought,
Yes common sense tells this to me –
There can be naught without a Deity.

By common sense the choice is mine –
To give this power a name divine,
To me it makes no sense at all –
Without a God on which to call.

To this I know some can't relate –
With common sense some can debate,
Their views of life that give relief –
The pros and cons of their belief.

But in these thoughts I offer you –
This common sense I now review,
This gift of life I live on earth –
If here by chance has little worth.

Creation, life, from a Godly power –
A joyous gift only God can shower,
To me it's clear, to me it's plain –
That only God can life explain.

As with my common sense explore –
The things on earth that total score,
As thoughts with common sense extend –
My life with God – not chance – does blend.

01-06-1994

Happy 5oth Birthday Greetings to my brother-in-law is next.

Dear Bill,

I think I know the way you feel –
So I hope you find this no big deal,
But the calendar to me does show –
That you're coming up on the big five O.

On January 22nd you'll turn a page –
That takes you closer to --- old age,
Although old age hard to define –
It's surely past age twenty-nine.

I think on that we both agree –
That we're beyond that – you and me,
That we accept the basic truth –
We're past that span of life – our youth.

But I'm not here age to compare –
For of your age we're both aware,
We know how many years gone by –
And just how quickly they did fly.

In all my years, now sixty-three –
The flow of life makes clear to me,
That age to birthdays do not bind –
For age is clearly – state of mind.

So with this rhyme to you I say –
I'm thankful you were born that day,
And though half a hundred seems a lot –
HAPPY BIRTHDAY BILL – it's really not.

Happy Birthday

01-13-94

Yes, more miscellaneous thoughts follow.

Peace

Sometimes there comes a peace –
from deep inside my soul,
It penetrates my senses –
and makes my Spirit whole.

With a mystical, gentle persuasion –
it overwhelms my mind,
With vision of truth, life eternal –
sensation of joy that I find.

Overcomes me with depth of emotion –
core of my being does astound,
It surpasses all my understanding –
this oneness with life so profound.

I'm subdued from the force of that power –
the perfection of love un-denied,
And I write this to show the relation –
God controls when my soul opens wide.

01-14-1994

This next to my daughter & son-in-law's new computer.

Dr. FAX

I covet your Four-Eighty-Six DX –
With its buttons & whistles, modem, FAX,
And your Laser printer I covet too –
I want them so badly don't know what to do.

I think I'll come get them, I will not delay –
Cause I want them, I want them, and right away,
Yes I'm gonna get them, I want them right now –
Except there's one problem – I don't know how.

I could use my influence, my wealth and my clout –
To get to Seattle during time you're both out,
I know where you live – I've been there before –
And I know would be easy to get through the door.

Oh wow! this is great, I'll go on with the plan –
Cause I sure want to do this as fast as I can,
I want your computer, and I want it real bad –
For this two-eighty-six is too slow, makes me mad.

With this ancient computer, I know you relate –
I remember, I remember, how we both it frustrate,
Then after you left and the hard disk I clean –
It began to torment me – this relic machine.

I'm a victim of progress, the victim of change –
The thought of your computer my mind does derange,
I want it, I need it, and you Griffiths' beware –
When your computer is missing - you'll know I've been there!!!!

01-15-1994

This next is self-explanatory with a school event of my
grandson's being the focus.

AJ

There's a handsome young boy – whose name is AJ,
Who has lots of fun – with his school mates in play,
He thinks Ninja Turtles – with bad guys compete,
As they jump in the air, twirl around, kick their feet.

Well one day at school – this young boy so fair,
He kicked with his feet and he jumped in the air,
Like his hero the Ninja – his friends he would show,
That the tricks of the Ninja – he also did know.

He knew all their secrets – he knew how to win,
So he act like a Ninja – with a kick to the shin,
But unlike the Ninja – his school mates were real,
And the pain from his kick, OUCH!, they could feel.

Then golly, his teacher – it made her quite sad,
For she knew her fair student – was good and not bad,
But to teach him a lesson – from his actions to learn,
His "Badge of Good Merit" – she made him return.

Now AJ's very smart – and he's really quite good,
And the result of his actions – he well understood,
Once more he began – all the nice things to do,
So his "Badge of Good Merit" – again could renew.

I know that in this – he is bound to succeed,
For AJ is the greatest – in action and deed,
You've probably guessed it – as my tale is done,
That AJ, this Angel – is of course --- my Grandson.

01-17-1994
Hot Springs, Ar
Majestic Hotel

I LOVE Southwest Air Lines.   I wrote this in flight to pass time
and did send it to them.

Southwest Air Lines

Some call it the "Cattle Company" –
This airline known as Southwest,
And sometimes when you fly it –
It puts you to the test.

There are no seat assignments –
You get into a line,
And at the tick counter –
A number they assign.

Then like cattle being driven –
They herd you through the door,
Stampede you down the aisle –
Till seats there are no more.

They boast of their fine service –
Airplanes filled with love,
But what they fail to mention –
They load you with a shove.

Then once upon the airplane –
For an aisle or window seat,
With some aggressive travelers –
You really must compete.

Come on Southwest Airlines –
In your high profile campaign,
I think you're overstating –
That you're the company plane.

I'd choose a mode more personal –
Flying with more class,
I'd never have to worry –
About a boarding pass.

I send this silly missive –
To try to let you know,
If today my first experience –
To another line would go.

Flight from Love to Austin –
On third plane we went,
With confusion in the terminal –
Too many hours were spent.

Finally got me back to Austin –
St the fading of the daylight,
And to ease my deep frustration –
Wrote this note to you in flight.

Herb I take the time to tell you –
You sit on top of the heap,
You still run a damn good airline –
Best of all you're really – CHEAP!!!

01-17-1994

This next I wrote should be very obvious and understandable. It was to my wife who will always be my VALENTINE.

Be My Valentine

I know you know I'm glad your mine –
That I want you to be my Valentine –
But tonight I have the urge to compose –
A tribute of love in written prose.

Since poetry is my biggest affliction –
Prose it seems is a contradiction –
For prose is described as commonplace –
With no meter or rhyme in it to trace.

Well you know that my logic is perverse –
Not only when my thoughts in verse –
Unimaginative, dull, mundane, direct -
So prose may be idiom quite correct.

But that's not really important to me –
Matters not if it's prose or poetry –
Poetry or prose, as I write every line –
I want you to please ---
BE MY VALENTINE!!!

02-06-1994

More Valentine thoughts follow, but this time to good friends.

Valentine Thoughts

This tray and this dish – since the last time we met,
Have been visible in my car – so we wouldn't forget,
So we wouldn't forget – to return them to you,
Along with our thanks – that's the least we could do.

We got them last year – at the class party we shared,
Though you couldn't stay long – good food you prepared,
Christmas cheer at the Mills' – the rest at our house,
Where we ate your fine food – then till late did carouse.

Yes Mary and Herb – the Faith Class thanks you a lot,
For friendship and love – best – the food that we got,
These things late returning – your food so divine,
Make you both the prime candidates – to be our --- Valentine !!!

02-12-1994

The next was written following a presentation made to our Sunday School Class by a good friend who was deeply involved with the Twelve Step Program at the counseling level.

Twelve Step

I write this poem as a way to express –
my thoughts on Twelve Step Presentation,
For people in need I am glad it is there –
to assist in their dire situation.

But the Twelve Step program is not for all –
for many it may not be needed,
That's not to say the goal of the plan –
by all in some way should be heeded.

Most that I've known, of course not all –
use a reasoned introspection,
The path they take in this troubled world –
is passage of their selection.

The reality of life gives no certain way –
that applies to all the masses,
There is not one plan can suit all needs –
for the many and varied classes.

Still the Twelve Step program I must admit –
is a plan we all can admire,
Giving aid to those who need it the most –
if improving is their desire.

When life complex and burdens are great –
the balance of living awry,
The Twelve Step program to some reaches out –
it helps them to understand why.

Then once understood their Spirits renewed –
move away from sin and resentment,
Each step they now take if no turning back –
returns them to God and contentment.

Yes God is the answer to all that we know –
to our joys our pain and our sorrow,
And Twelve Step program for some a good way –
to proceed from today to tomorrow.

But Twelve Step program again not for all –
in harmony and peace some are growing,
Accepting this gift, the wonders of life –
and the bounty of love God bestowing.

I have not the need to expose to the world –
all the hurt from my sin to set free,
I live with my past, pray forgiveness will come –
from Grace – only God — offers me.

02-13-1994

I flew an Engineering Team to Biloxi, Mississippi for one of their scheduled visits there. As I was waiting for them outside where we were to have dinner, I was overwhelmed by the sunset and began the poem below that was finished in my hotel room later.

Sunset

As I await my friends for dinner –
at a restaurant by the shore,
There in Gulfport Mississippi –
where we all have been before.

As my mind on them was playing –
they were reason I was there,
And my mood was one of pleasure –
in the purpose that we share.

There came to me a warm feeling –
as the sun set in the west,
As the dark of night came slowly –
easing daylight to its rest.

From the beauty in the sunset –
the hue of red in sky,
There came a sense of reverence –
that I could not deny.

Yes it stole into my senses –
no room for daily stress,
Only silent joy and wonder –
from peace of its caress.

My friends disturbed the aura –
the magic spell I was in,
But returned the mood of pleasure –
as evening with friends did begin.

02-17-1994
Gulfport, Ms - at the Best Western Seaway Inn

This next came to me from an accumulation of notes and memories that I put into rhyme. During my flying career I was required by the FAA, and Insurance needs, to keep my proficiency and flying skills up to high standards. To do that, on an annual basis, I would go to a training program in St. Louis. It was during that time period that I managed to arrange to meet my family in Bloomington, Ill. and that resulted in ---

Weekend

This weekend in St. Louis –
with life was I imbued,
From hugs of my granddaughters –
by love was I renewed.

The sound of impish laughter –
the twinkle in their eye,
The vibrancy of these children –
gave strength could not deny.

Their rowdy play together –
my patience they explored,
But the innocence of childhood –
my energies restored.

I savored the attention –
so long had been without,
And I reveled at the beauty –
of having them about.

Their need for my attention –
their silly, giggly play,
Enforce in me the knowledge –
that children rule the day.

They test restraining limits –
they're told to stay within,
As they go through growing process –
of changing world are in.

From Bloomington to St. Louis –
their manner unrestrained,
And we bonded well together –
as each other entertained.

The cheeseburger for Halie –
with ketchup made her mad,
Then with silly sense of humor –
she joked that it was bad.

But Heather shared her chicken –
and French fries were enough,
To keep that part of the journey –
from getting really rough.

At one moment was distracted –
Sprite somehow got spilled,
Turns out was I who did it –
of course the girls were thrilled.

Also Heather had some excitement –
with Hot Air Balloon had fun,
A balloon that I had not sighted –
we argued – ooops she won.

Ah – they sang songs from Oklahoma –
Meet Me In St. Louis too,
And the journey went too quickly –
as my spirits they renew.

In St. Louis we came together –
Mary and Gary, Samantha, Mi Mi,
Halie and Heather had to go swimming –
before their Mi Mi did see.

Samantha of course needs attention –
not a baby but her binky a need,
It had best be around when she wants it –
or all comes to a halt won't proceed.

The pool, the zoo, Arch and the riverboat –
the meal at Friday's we shared,
We were a family enjoying a weekend –
to best things in life all compared.

Now I'm back from my journey in Austin –
but last night while up in flight,
I passed some time in fond memory –
my thoughts on an envelope to write.

I sit with my thoughts at the computer –
these feelings of love to sort out,
To remind me some day in the future –
of the weekend and what life's about.

03-13/14-1994
Mostly written on SW Flight from St. Louis to Austin.

Yes, more of my miscellaneous thoughts on Reflections follow.

Reflections

I see myself as a reflection –
that mirrors the substance of me,
Reflecting the stuff I am made of –
my persona that people will see.

My reflection is constantly changing –
for intensity of light never same,
There is change from time of conception –
and passage of time bears the blame.

For all things by time are illumined –
essential to put things in view,
Time – time the light of creation –
God's Creation that made life ensue.

Yes, my image is cast from reflections –
ancestry, environment, choice, chance,
How I stand in the light gives direction –
to reflections that I can enhance.

So substance of life is reflection –
illuminating the wrong and the right,
Was Created by God this reflection –
when commanded He, "Let there be light".

03-21-1994

To my wife for her birthday follows.

Birthday

My darling Myrtle Anne – I'll do the best I can,
With the writing I now do – to show my love for you.
I know it may be trite – the poem I now write,
But with the gifts you find – I hope that you won't mind.

The perfume and birthstone – reflect your image shown,
Not only just to me – but to all with eyes to see.
Of course you are no saint – but then I also ain't,
That really matters not – with all the love we got.

I'd buy you a birthday card – but there is no other bard,
That ever could reveal – the love for you I feel.
No one can take your place – in thoughts that I embrace,
And I hope my love is shown – with the perfume and birthstone.

Yes, I love you Myrtle Anne – in most every way I can,
You are beautiful and great – much to young to be fifty-eight.

With all my love --- HAPPY BIRTHDAY!!!

03-23-1994

The following were thoughts written on a Sunday sermon.

Will Be Done

To me all things done by God's Will,
God's plan and purpose to fulfill,
When term of life has all been run,
It will be found God's will be done.

God's will be done --- self-evident,
For all is wrought from God's intent,
God's will alone we all must heed,
God's will alone makes life proceed.

There is no power, no greater force,
Can change the flow of Godly course,
God's will be done since time began,
God's will created all things – man.

God's will be done – "Let there be light",
With that command made day and night,
God's will be done – the power of choice,
God's will be done – oh joy --- rejoice.

God's will be done – God's saving Grace,
The will of God – with love embrace,
God's will be done – will set me free,
The will of God --- gives hope to me.

God's will and time my being share,
All that I am is in their care,
With reverent thought they are the same,
God's will and time --- oh Holy Name.

God's will and time cannot refute,
With Grace of God stand resolute,
God's will be done gives hope sublime,
God's will be done and in God's time.

God's will and time are intertwined,
Within my thoughts they are aligned,
If time should cease – oh perish thought,
God's will be done – would be for naught.

03-28-1994

Following the thought process of the previous, I wrote the next.

Thoughts

The human body as it must –
Will someday end and turn to dust,
Someday submit to final breath –
And acquiesce to terms of death.

The terms of death that now begin –
From out the body they were in,
Depend upon the thoughts once chose –
Before life on this earth did close.

To laws of physics the body tied –
Those laws could never be denied,
But mind from laws was ever free –
And that's the way was meant to be.

The body process well explained –
By earthly pleasures entertained,
But power of thought within the mind –
Comes from a source we cannot find.

A source from out this atmosphere –
Metaphysical force that's always near,
To every mind is thought a part –
Eternal source in Spiritual heart.

When life on earth in the body done –
To another form will thoughts now run,
When out of the body find new norm –
As it acclimates to ethereal form.

Thought process is an eternal thing –
To all of life does meaning bring ,
The power of thought is always on –
And what life on earth is built upon.

So guard this sanctity of thought –
That guides the body in which caught,
When the body returns to nature's care –
Miracle of thought will still be there.

04-05-1994

The next poem was written to a good Doctor friend of the
families I flew for. Following a series of flights, as he was
departing, he offered his hand in a warm handshake. I was
surprised at his sincere pleasantry and generosity.

Dear Dr. Cain

Generosity

When you offered me your hand to shake –
And I your hand in mine did take,
It came as some surprise to me –
Your expression of generosity.

I hold the highest thought of you –
The caring things I've seen you do,
The tactfulness of what you say –
The manner of your subtle way.

Your breadth of sterling quality –
Your depth of rare gentility,
No one who knows you can contest –
Especially those who know you best

Your handshake made with good intent –
I accept as honored compliment,
To your generosity beyond the norm –
I now return --- in poetic form.

With warm regards and thanks.

04-07-1994
Majestic Hotel Cottage
Hot Springs, Ar

This next poem was as well written in Hot Springs. They were
thoughts following visits with a 96 year old dear friend I was
close to at the Hotel. She had never been married and claimed to
have lived a perfect life with no regrets. She was not well and I
visited her first at her Nursing Home and finally at the St.
Joseph's Hospital where she died soon after.

The poem tells the story.

Play the Part

This poem I write to Mary Quinn –
She's put me in this mood I'm in,
A mood I'll try now to explain –
Reflective mood that brings me pain.

Her strife with age I've seen before –
A part of life that I deplore,
Web of time in which she's caught –
The curse of age – jumbled thought.

My person now she does not know –
Her mind goes back to long ago,
I'm someone now from out her past –
She's grateful I've come back at last.

Through me the past she does explore –
The people she has known before,
She wanders back into her youth –
I play the part hold back the truth.

I found her sitting in a chair –
Upon her face look of despair,
Her body weak, so frail and worn –
She looked so lifeless and forlorn.

But as I walked into the room –
Was gone from her, her look of gloom,
She came alive in memory –
Of whom she thought she saw in me.

She saw in me a person dear –
In memory now she brought him near,
It seemed to make her very glad –
The memories of this man she had.

She asked if Joan knew I was there –
And if she knew of our affair,
So many things she told me of –
With joy relived a past of love.

To her no longer was I --- me –
Another man in me did see,
From out her past a long lost friend –
I had no choice but to pretend.

I played the part of loved one Bill –
As portions of her memory fill,
And oh I think would break her heart –
If I opted not to play that part.

Her tales were rambling and confused –
By my unclear answers she was amused,
Her love for Bill to me revealed –
As I my pain from her concealed.

I tell her that I understand –
Caress her cheek and touch her hand,
I perform the role impressed on me –
So that Mary - Bill, not me, would see.

I found that Mary could console –
As long as I stayed in the role,
I paid the price with Mary there –
So she with Bill the past could share.

I played part well, she did believe –
But as it must, came time to leave,
I left her sitting in the chair –
Upon her face returned despair.

Yes life goes on I went my way –
Back to my world myself to play,
From Mary's world did I depart –
And left a piece --- of aching heart.

04-08/09-1994
Hot Springs, Ark. - Majestic Hotel Cottage

My thoughts to a High School friend of my wife follow.

Dear Frances,

Reunion

You caught me at home passing some time,
Reviewing thoughts I've put into rhyme.
You reminded me of a poem I once wrote,
On a dinner napkin my thoughts to denote.

That was in Harlingen some years ago,
During a reunion dinner as you well know.
Specifics of poem of course can't recall,
I gave it to someone to read to you all.

I watched the activity, heard y'all converse,
And my observations I put into verse.
The nostalgia pervading really was great,
As friends in reunion together relate.

Events of school days were bantered about,
And humorous awards to a few handed out.
So many good topics from which to select,
I'm sure that the poem all that did reflect.

Yes the poem I wrote was fun at the time,
It was such a good group to put into rhyme.
The relationships strong were easy to see,
And reflections of memory a pleasure to me.

Now you asked if another poem I'd write,
Since your 25th reunion gave me such delight.
With this your 40th I want you to know,
I look forward to seeing another big show.

04-11-1994

P.S.

A slumber party at y'alls age,
I'm sure would fill a poet's page,
A hell of a poem I know I'd write,
But I doubt you'd let me spend the night.

This next was sent to two friends of mine. I add the note preceding it,
to explain thoughts I was attempting to express.

Dear Joyce and Gus,

I send this to let you know that Myrtle and I are thinking of you and offer love and prayers for your mother. Following the service Wednesday, I had need to put my thoughts into a poem. As you know, I use poetry as an outlet for my emotions which at most times I keep to myself. I hope this poem expresses to you my respect for you both, and how meaningful the service was to me.

Presence

Our encounter in church foyer –
before the service start,
The strength of your composure –
was enlightening to my heart.

In the tone of conversations –
the depth of love did show,
Respect for your dear mother –
who I've met but didn't know.

Then Jim through his fine sermon –
made her goodness come alive,
And as I listened to the service –
another presence did arrive.

To all there is a time and a season –
a time to be born and to die,
This passage of time most fitting –
a truth that no one can deny.

As was read, this powerful presence –
came into the church today,
A gentle, commanding presence –
nearly took my breath away.

In the aura of what there pervading –
a mother's love was found,
And the arms of this Holy presence –
her Spirit did surround.

The person there sitting beside me –
with the beauty of her voice,
Reinforced the feeling of presence –
as through hymns she now rejoice.

I'm so sure this Spiritual presence –
to the church, the service came,
To comfort those here gathered –
in Jesus and your mother's name.

Yes I came to honor your mother –
to share in your loss and grief,
And found there embracing your mother –
God's presence that gave me --- relief.

04-13-1994

Next was something I wrote to help a friend who wanted to
introduce singing to the Rotary Club of which I was a member.
I came up with this rhyme to, " Home, Home On the Range".

Rotarians

Oh give me a home where Rotarians roam –
Where their motto is rule of the day,
Where the things they believe –
Are the things they achieve –
In the highest Rotarian way.

Home – home in the fold –
Where we meet in a unified way,
Where we all join as one –
With good works and good fun –
And our fellowship honors the day.

I tell you my friend, as your motto extend –
With expressions of what you believe,
If you join hand in hand –
Stay unbowed do not bend –
Then your goals you are bound to achieve.

Home – home in the fold –
Where we meet in a unified way,
Where we all join as one –
With good works and good fun –
And our fellowship honors the day.

To a Rotary strong lift your voices in song –
Sing it loud so that all who hear know,
In this Rotary fold –
You are proud to belong –
And your legions forever will grow.

Home – home in the fold –
Where we meet in a unified way,
Where we all join as one –
With good works and good fun –
And our fellowship honors the day.

05-15-1994

The next was to a dear friend who gave me a pamphlet that was
on an organization she participated in at the University. She
was an educator with high credentials. She was as well, a fellow
Rotarian.   Poem began with a brief note to her –

Dear Millie,

I was reviewing this little pamphlet you gave me once,
and, of course, came up with the following:

Explorers

We are explorers – and we find it most compelling,
The frontiers of our time – human consciousness rappelling,
In our quest – our vision for humanity,
We must integrate – both science and spirituality.

And in so doing – ever mindful in our living,
Be connected – to each other, the earth and giving,
Yes in giving – what to inner self is true,
All our talents – so our being we renew.

05-22-1994

This next was again to the Rotary Club I was a member of.

Dear Wayne,

In response to your call Wednesday, I offer the following ------

Volunteer

The Rotary - it's very clear –
Depends on help that's volunteer,
Can't operate on crass demand –
To further goals it takes in hand.

Volunteers with what they know –
It takes to make a project go,
If a Rotary goal is meant to be –
It takes volunteers in harmony.

For all club efforts to succeed –
The volunteers a leader need,
A leader at their beck and call –
A leader such as you – Wayne Hall.

The University Club with intellect –
As President you did select,
To take the reins from leader Royal –
Who with brilliance all did spoil.

We know you'll have a different style –
With wit and song and ready smile,
With energy and suave and grace –
We're sure you'll set the proper pace.

We'll join with you in coming year –
To answer call as a volunteer,
We'll do the very best we can –
To further goals that club may plan.

So Wayne I take your talk to heart –
I volunteer to do my part,
I hope this gives to you a lift –
And of course look forward --- to my gift!

05-27-94

These next two were written for dear and close friends from our days in the Air Force. Dick had retired from a very distinguished career as a Full Colonel. After retirement from the Air Force, the Austin School District, and his students, were specially fortunate in his productive time with them teaching at the High School level. His wife Sue, planned his second retirement party to which my wife and I were invited.

Toast

We have gathered me and you –
From the covert actions of Sue,
So let's offer up a toast –
To our scheming, conniving host.

With secrets she kept from Dick –
She got us here to Salt Lick,
For what is the main event –
Dick's second retirement.

When his Air Force career was done –
Dick's second career begun,
Now although Dick Bower is tough –
With the system he's had enough.

Next toast then with three cheers –
To Dick his distinguished careers,
Lift your glass and raise it high –
To this Colonel, great teacher –
one hell of a guy!!!

06-03-1994

Sue and You

To Sue and you Dick Bower –
These gifts on you we shower,
The sweets of course are for Sue –
And the beaded seat thing for you.

From Lamme's the truffles came –
On Relax the Back the beaded seat blame,
These token gifts on my own did find –
With you're retirement well in mind.

Now the gifts — I opted to choose –
So Myrtle --- you can't accuse,
She'd buy something snazzy, exotic –
Depending on mood maybe even erotic.

But the gifts from us both that you see –
And this stilted verse written by me,
Are to tell Sue and you - that we like you a lot --
You are two of the very best friends that we got!!!

06-04-1994

Amazing Grace is for me a beautiful hymn. The word wretch
though troubled me. So, I took the liberty of changing the
wording some. What follows is my third re-write version.

Amazing Grace

Amazing Grace it comforts me –
The music fills my soul,
From world of sin it sets me free –
It makes my Spirit whole.

A new found peace comes over me –
There's naught in life to fear.
I feel God's strength, tranquility –
When sound of hymn I hear.

Is not the words that comfort me –
Though words they may apply,
But sound of hymn, God's symphony –
Brings calm I can't deny.

How sweet the calm that blesses me –
When God with me does share,
That He in me no wretch doth see,
And that for me does care.

Amazing Grace oerpowers me –
With faith the future face,
I sense a joy that's yet to be –
Through God's ---- Amazing Grace!!!

06-06-1994

This next was written during my wife's 40th Harlingen High
School reunion that was held at the Ramada Inn in San Antonio.

Unchanging

It's your Fortieth reunion – and fifteen years since when,
You were in Harlingen together – now in San Antonio again.
I join in your reunion – here at Airport Ramada Inn,
As you renew teen-age relations – fond memories begin.

I watch and hear the greetings – "You haven't changed at all",
And I wonder with good humor – just what you all recall.
I look on happy faces – expressions most sincere,
Try to analyze the vision – through the eyes of people here.

I am sure you see this classmate – this person from your past,
With the vision you remember – from good memories that last.
The vision from your memory – and what time did rearrange,
With respect and love transfigured –unnoticed is all the change.

Once again as in last reunion – by warmth and love are caught,
In the lesson of your greeting – with your goodness I am taught.
I am taught though time is fleeting – and years go quickly by,
It is love that shapes the image – as is seen by heart and eye.

So Red Cardinals here around me – to you all I raise a glass,
In a toast to your reunion – to the goodness of your class.
And to Hostess Frances Shannon – wonderful work she's done,
Drink to unchanging beauty – in the hearts of all she has won.

Cheers
06-18-1994

Logic

When words of Bible we explore,
Our basic logic must ignore,
We really have to overlook,
What seems illogic in the book.

With passages that we select,
We have to curb our intellect,
Although some writings seem absurd,
We must not question Bible's word.

The Bible's meaning must be taught,
By scholars with religious thought,
The words from Bible simple, plain,
Their deeper meaning to explain.

To me it's more than passing strange,
That our logic we must rearrange,
That a scholar the Bible must relate,
For a God who all does dominate.

No – it takes no scholar God to teach,
It takes a soul and mind to reach,
To reach to God through simple thought,
With logic, faith to then be taught.

The Bible though I won't assail,
But on my logic will prevail,
For God leaves not to mortal man,
To teach His word catch as catch can.

God speaks to us much more direct,
And gives us Grace if we select,
Through faith and prayer within our mind,
Eternal Truth ------ with logic find.

07-03-94

Thought at my nephew Steve's wedding in Puerto Rico.

As One

Before this place we leave –
A toast to Lil and Steve –
On wedding rings they trade –
With vows of love they made.

And their vows we know for sure –
Will forever and ever endure –
For in Steve and Lil we see –
The support of their family.

Great love forms the strong foundation –
That is basis for their relation –
The goodness of Steve and Lil –
Comes from love that their family instill.

Stephen Coats, Lil Pabon now as one –
Your new family unit begun –
Look to those who in love made this day –
And success for your future – now pray.

A TOAST !!!!!

07-09-1994
San Juan, Puerto Rico

They Came

From Puerto Rico and the U.S.A. –
Two families met in this church today –
Two families with traditions strong –
Shared with each other prayer and song.

In two languages was the service said –
In Spanish and English the Pastor read –
With Steve and Lil there side by side –
They vowed with the Bible to abide.

So within this sacred, holy place –
Two lives as one God's love did grace –
Through vows of marriage two became –
One family unit with one name.

Steve Coats, Lil Pabon together here –
To make intentions loud and clear –
To this, Christ's Church, came to be wed –
With Grace of God to share one bed.

When Pastor pronounced them man and wife –
They entered in their married life –
Lives now merged with scriptural start –
In a holy union share one heart.

Marylou and Fred, Nilda and Ramon –
With surname Coats, and surname Pabon –
Gave love of family for them to hold –
That is more precious than silver or gold.

Two families joined with Steve and Lil –
To witness the passing of God's Will –
With prayers and faith in Jesus Name –
In joy of life --- two families came.

07-09-1994
San Juan, Puerto Rico
Regency Hotel

More miscellaneous thoughts of the moment with the strong
urge to write follow.

Healing

In the vortex of time I am caught,
A process to all things consuming,
In my mind at this moment is brought,
A concept of time most illuming.

In the passage of moment is found,
That time is the factor controlling,
The whole of my being does surround,
Hand of time is elixir consoling.

I know that this moment won't last,
For time is a force most compelling,
That makes of each moment the past,
Ever forward life's purpose propelling.

I find God in my concept of time,
The Grace of God's love there revealing,
And the pain that inspired this rhyme,
Overcome by times power of --- healing.

08-20/21-1994
Houston, Tx (Motel 6)

Thoughts to pass time with the family on vacation.

Family

I found myself upon the beach –
My wife and children in my reach –
My children's children as before –
Joined there with me on sandy shore.

To Island House on Padre Isle –
I went with loved ones for a while –
To share some joy and summer fun –
Upon the beach with surf and sun.

I watched at times with sense of awe –
The family traits in those I saw –
A smile, a look – blond hair, blue eyes –
Reflected the mystery of hereditary ties.

Life's procreative powers it did reflect –
How the mix of genes somehow select –
The form and shape of what will be –
The generational look of a family.

There on the beach oh was I blessed –
By family bonds my mind caressed –
No greater gift on earth could be –
Than the gift of love from family.

Begun 07-20-1994, Padre Island - finished 08-30-1994 Austin, Tx

Next collection of words, are my thoughts on reading the book
"The Arrow of Time" by Peter Coveney and Roger Highfield.

Plan

The laws of physics now in place –
Define how objects move in space,
The laws to which they must relate –
Their present, past and future state.

Around the heavens they now go –
With laws of physics that we know,
Their spatial movements can compute –
With Newton's laws so absolute.

All his laws have proven true –
A clear and easy thing to do,
And his formulas to time are tied –
Thus time to all, to all allied.

Now Einstein's theories also show –
Mass, speed, and time together go,
That near great mass there is a trend –
The path of light rays now to bend.

That force and mass by some design –
The heavenly bodies do align,
That every mass and every force –
Affects each on celestial course.

If a mass accelerates in flight –
And it approaches speed of light,
Times measurement begins to slow –
And the size of mass begins to grow.

Thus time and motion intertwined –
Determine how all things aligned,
Force and mass and speed and time –
Command all space as words do rhyme.

For valid measurements to get –
There has to be a standard set,
In the space of all infinity –
One certain constant there must be.

The laws of physics won't endure –
Unless there is a constant sure,
A constant can't be rearranged –
One measure certain, sure, unchanged.

Time the constant now is used –
But by speed is time confused,
At great speed time will change –
The laws of physics rearrange.

It is seen that out in space –
New stars are put into place,
In the heavens they are born –
Our sky and Cosmos to adorn.

And in space there are also found –
Black holes that do confound,
Great whirlpools in the sky –
Our understandings now defy.

Though their presence we can trace –
They are mysteries out in space,
Where all time and mass and light –
Are consumed and out of sight.

Seems as all towards holes proceed –
With an ever increasing speed,
That each mass will quickly grow –
Time may stop and backward go.

But as yet there is little proof –
Of these holes within our roof,
Where dimensions seem to blend –
And time slows then comes to end.

Laws of physics may be no more –
There may find another score,
Another dimension to astound –
The metaphysical may now abound.

In that place when liberated –
Find the source of why created,
For once thru that blackened hole –
Be reborn as Spirit --- Soul.

There to find a new relation –
With the source of all Creation,
Where in Spirit, not as man –
Find fulfillment with God's Plan.

09-??-1994

This next is a poem I faxed to Liz Carpenter. We at that time, briefly exchanged communications together.

Dear Liz –

Liz

I've just watched you on TV –
And what a joy for me –
To see a great lady I know –
On a C-Span televised show.

It was good to see you there –
As again with me you share –
Your thoughts that give delight –
On a book that you did write.

I smiled with you when you told –
How "Bay at the Moon" did unfold –
It was easy to see your pleasure –
Of a Society you obviously treasure.

And my thoughts you did provoke –
As with Bryan Lamb you spoke –
And feelings you did enhance –
Of Big Bend and Spiral Dance.

Though our politics don't agree –
You've endeared yourself to me –
And your book I am sure will share –
The inner warmth that is there.

The book I know will be great –
For you've proven you can relate –
The contents of life you select –
In a manner that's clear and direct.

Tomorrow your book I will buy –
But once more I thought I would try –
To give you my thoughts in a poem –
And send it, via FAX, to your home.

10-23-1994

Excuse the silliness, but I did enjoy watching you tonight!!!

Dear Liz

Rest

I have your book and think it's great –
The special way that you relate,
Your book on "Unplanned Parenthood" –
Is one of substance --- really good!

The style and wit with which you write –
Is source of pleasure – brings delight –
You have a gift that's held by few –
As you express those thoughts in you.

With all the memoirs in your book –
You take us in your heart to look –
You show your tough and softer side –
With warmth and candor un-denied.

My deep respect you've already won –
Long time before your book begun –
When at La Jitas in Big Bend –
Your hand of friendship you extend.

So it comes as no surprise to me –
You're blessings on these children three –
Confirms the stuff of which you're made –
The role in life you've richly played.

So hope you hear from Ed McMahon –
Or from Reader's Digest on other plan –
I wish for you in life the very best –
For Golly Liz ---- you need a rest !!!

10-31-1994

Liz - I won't bother you anymore with this stuff, but did
want you to know how   much I enjoyed knowing more
about you and those who influenced your life
What follows is something I wrote and sent to a good friend.

I had flown some hunters to Falfurias in South Texas. While
there at the motel reading the San Antonio Express, I came upon
an article, How may heroes in a life?, that was written by an old
Air Force friend of mine Tony Weissgarber. I took time then
and wrote the following that I did send to him.

Dear Tony,Read that nice article and couldn't help but write the
following. Give Myrtle and my love to Ruth as well as to your
neighbors Jim and Marsha Humphries.

Hero

I enjoyed what I read in the paper –
The perception of heroes to you,
On the stuff your heroes were made of –
The example was set by those few.

Three men who on your life impacted –
And emotions in you they incite,
By their actions and moral convictions –
Enforcing the wrong and the right.

You were favored to have them as heroes –
To learn and be shaped by the three,
And their influence makes of you a hero –
In the person you turned out to be.

Was a tribute to serve in your company –
To know you as a leader and friend,
To share in the wealth of your goodness –
With the example in life you extend.

So Tony I reflect for a moment –
On persons I've known in the past,
Those people with a depth of integrity –
Who by deeds can as heroes be cast.

You and your neighbor Jim Humphries –
Are two that come quickly to mind,
Two men with a great sense of purpose –
The quality in heroes you find.

Now I'm sure that there must be two others –
Who see you as a hero of worth,
So with three you have surely accomplished –
The success you define on this earth.

But success is a hard thing to measure –
Is uncertain until life is done,
Only when you are judged by your Maker –
Will you know if success – truly won.

11-12-1994
Falfurias, Tx (Antlers Inn)

This next was something I sent to our local newspaper's
Letters to the Editor.

Dear Editor

Again you manage to provoke me to a poem. Must admit, since
the last election, I find myself in better humor with the content
of your paper. Thank you for presenting the other side. It helps
keep things in balance with me and I hope to reciprocate.

Out of Touch

Since the latest historical event –
When a political message was sent –
The Statesman thru your expression –
Continues with liberal impression.

Ben Sargent's cartoons of late –
Through the message he tries to create –
Show that his mindset still is caught –
In inflexible though humorous thought.

The proclivity he tries to invoke –
Makes your paper butt of the joke –
For it seems you both fail to see –
you're out of touch with majority.

11-16-1994

This next is a response I faxed to Liz Carpenter answering a fax
she had sent to me.

Dear Liz,

Thank you for your response. Knowing how busy you are with
all the demands for your time, make me even more appreciative.
I'm not sure we disagree too much on basic values, rather in the
method of achievement. I couldn't help but enjoy your limerick
and it may surprise you to know I agree, to some extent, on your
assessment --- HOWEVER; -----

The Dinosaur

Your limerick on Gramm, Gingrich, Dole –
With our national debt in a hole –
Reflects push to the right –
For budget that's tight –
By majority that made that their goal.

Was a dinosaur who this did provoke –
By thrust of philosophy spoke –
It is fair to denote –
A historical vote –
And the reign of the donkey now broke.

But with you in a way I agree –
What in some politicians I see,
If we followed your tack –
Family values took back –
Then our nation would whole again be.

11-18-1994

This next was another experience with grandchildren.

Leaps & Bounds

One Saturday to Leaps & Bounds –
four children found their way,
To share with playmates in that place –
the magic bonds of play.

Through maze of tunnels, ramps and slides –
they leap, they bound they run,
They howl with screams of gusto loud –
in an atmosphere of fun.

On hands and knees I joined with them –
Samantha, Heather and Hailey,
To find what hidden in the maze –
that set their spirits free.

Where came the joy, the shine in eyes –
the freedom of their mind,
The endless source of energy –
that only children find.

But what I found within the maze –
was not the answer sought,
I did not find the thrill of play –
to little children brought.

I found instead the truth of life –
as maze with me engage,
That it for children is designed –
it told me – "Act your age!!!".

11-26-1994
Leaps & Bounds at the Bullins (Spring, Tx)

This next was to Wayne Hall, our Rotary Club President. The
previous week he gave a large party at the Radison Hotel for his
company at which he did a superb Elvis Presley act.

Elvis

These thoughts were in my mind –
As I watched you bump and grind –
As you strut around the stage –
Elvis image to engage.

You looked dandy all in white –
For sore eyes you were a sight –
And the lyrics you expound –
In that setting were most sound.

I could just see Elvis smile –
As you imitate his style –
As you slurred your words and more –
Shook your hips around the floor.

Yes your act is one of class –
A great voice and limber a __ –
A part of you I didn't know –
You revealed in Christmas show.

So I thank you for the chance –
Another side of you to glance –
And with this silly verse relate –
That your party Wayne --- was great!!!

12-07-1994

This next was to a dear friend in our Sunday School Faith Class.

Dear Gus – Missed you and Joyce in class this morning. Jean
gave an outstanding book review that I know you both would
have enjoyed. She is an outstanding class leader and had us
laughing and learning. Thought you might enjoy what I wrote
this morning before going to class that was prompted by our
discussion last week. Myrtle wasn't too fond of it – -- said it
might offend some --- I don't know !!!

Teach

To Faith Class members all –
On you I make this call –
To you I now beseech –
This hallowed class to teach.

First would like to thank –
Those of you who rank –
With Andrew, Jim and Danny –
For getting off your fanny.

For taking time to share –
Through lessons you prepare –
With those of us who sit –
And harass you with our wit.

Yes Judy, Doreen and Jean –
Three more of those I mean –
Who joined with honored few –
Their thoughts with class review.

But respected leader Gus –
In talk with some of us –
Intending to impress –
The following express.

In Nineteen – ninety five –
If class to stay alive –
Must even teaching chore –
From nineteen – ninety four.

Each member in the class –
Must get up off their a__ –
To lead from center stage –
The class from there engage.

Now the calendar must fill –
If indeed we have the will –
Faith class to keep intact –
In Good FAITH we must react.

As thoughts to rhyme I blend –
I hope I don't offend –
I hope instead to see –
Faith Class in unity.

And I pledge to do my part –
As Ninety five we start –
To practice what I preach –
Sign the role and try to – teach.

12-11-1994

This next was again generated by my Rotary Club.

Potter

This tray I offer up today –
Is work of art that's made from clay –
Created by a neighbor friend –
Whose soul in all her work does blend.

Within this clay she did instill –
The essence of her Master skill –
Embodied in this tray of white –
Is a gentle nature gives delight.

Her grace and beauty known to me –
Is in this tray for all to see –
From gifted potter this work came –
And Rebecca Roberts is her name.

But tray is more than work of art –
Of all life's wonders it is part –
Creation's mysteries on review –
In splendorous things that people do.

So tray is something fine and grand –
The product of this potter's hand –
Was my good fortune in her to find –
A treasure of --- the highest kind.

12-14-1994

Previous poem was on a purchase for a Rotary raffle donation I was responsible to get. I felt something from my gifted neighbor would be appreciated, so I solicited her help. She was willing and, as always, most gracious in assisting me. I loved the tray and she agreed with my selection. Knowing it was for Rotary, she discounted the cost of the tray. She is a lady you all would be privileged to know. (Above was read at a club meeting)

The following was as well read at a club party shortly thereafter.

Rotary Toast

To the University Area Rotary – guests and members here,
I wish for you the very best – in this upcoming year.
I wish for you great happiness – the blessings of good health,
Warmth of friends and family – success and increased wealth.

I thank Wayne our president – Susie Ward, Brad Seals all those,
Who kept the club upon the track – from start of year to close.
Take this time to also thank – Susie Maloney, Carl and Jerry,
As well as Millie and Penny – who serve next year with Terry.

To University Club I raise a toast – join in with me to show,
The Rotary Spirit does prevail – and our membership will grow.

12-16-1994

It was that time of the year when icing during flight was a distinct threat at times. There were a few recent fatal incidents in that regard, prompting the wonderful families at the time that I flew for, to include a brief poem to me in their season's greetings. I could not resist the urge to respond with the following ----

Ice Not Nice

Your Christmas message did suffice –
To share with me a gift quite nice –
But it also was a neat device –
To share concerns you had of ice.

It's nice to know that you enjoy –
The pilot skills that I employ –
To fill the needs of Ann and Roy –
As well of those of Morin – Joy.

Now in this message I'll impart –
I take your message well to heart –
As Christmas Season we do start –
Of icing we will have no part.

From icing I will stay well clear –
So icing then you need not fear –
Now to you and families I hold dear –
Your Captain offers – CHRISTMAS CHEER!!!

Captain Tony Melli
12-19-1994

Thank you once more for your generous gift, but more
importantly for your friendship in a relationship I hold in the
highest. I loved the rhyme, the thoughts expressed, and the
personal touch of all.

As well, with the families I flew for, I always submitted an
annual report in rhyme on the status of the aircraft. I will
include this particular one in this book since it is rather
mundane and brought back to me more good memories in
getting my poems ready to publish. It follows:

Leo Plan

As year of Ninety-four is closed –
This annual report on you imposed –
All dollar figures shown to you –
The bottom line put on review.

Within the numbers that are shown –
Are costs for all the hours flown –
And the numbers that we analyze –
We find in them no big surprise.

Operations plan that we select –
Met most criterion we project –
The plus exceeded the minus slack –
Thus bottom line is in the black.

Comments then will be quite short –
There is no shock in the report –
In fact with year I'm quite content –
The money seems has been well spent.

However I must caution you –
Airplane systems far from new –
Avionics, airframe, all the rest –
Dollar reserves may put to test.

We want an airplane safe to fly –
So cost for maintenance can't deny –
I know with that you all agree –
And give your whole support to me.

I have done the very best I can –
To present to you a reasonable plan –
From known statistics to derive –
Operations plan for Ninety-five.

I hope the plan looks good to you –
An option that you choose to do –
Whatever your choice I make it clear –
You are all great people I hold dear.

Captain Tony Melli
12-31-1994

Here's to a good year in Ninety-five. I want to thank you for all
our years together. I appreciate your patience, goodness,
friendship, generosity and very special relationship.

The Rotary Club I was a member of was searching for a new
meeting place. The next was written and sent to our Club
President following a trial meeting at one of the locations.

Ambience

Last night at Wylie's where we met –
The food and service nice,
The setting as you might expect –
I guess was worth the price.

The meeting surely went quite well –
Club purposes attained,
And the reason for our being there –
By you was well explained.

I think that Wylie's fit the bill –
Or so it did appear,
For members seemed to well enjoy –
East 6th Street atmosphere.

The social time before we start –
The spirit of members all,
Gave to the bar a touch of class –
Made Wylie's place stand tall.

Yes Wylie's was a lot of fun –
From pledge to all the rest,
A meeting place can now compare –
To others we may test.

To analyze before we choose –
The food, the price and more,
The more that makes a club to grow –
Location and décor.

So I'll wait until we meet again –
In fairness then to see,
What will be best to meet the need –
Of the University Rotary.

Now please take this as it is meant –
Last thought I offer you,
The "ambience" in Wylie's place –
Is minimal --- in my view.

01-05-1995

This next was written to a good friend. Dear Jimmie - You
asked me Friday night if I would recite my thoughts in poetry
for the evening. There are those times I am able to do that, but I
have little control as to when. I had many thoughts on my mind
however, and share them now with you. I sincerely hope you
enjoy my thoughts of the night in poetry.

Mother's Love

The joy last night in you observed –
At St. Luke's Church was well deserved,
From you there came an outward glow –
Your mother's love to me did show.

I'm glad you shared your joy with me –
That marriage in your family,
The bonding of two souls in love –
Through a union blessed by God above.

Your face to me did well express –
True measure of your happiness,
The mother's love within your heart –
On all your actions played a part.

It was in the church there everywhere –
Then at Tarrytown continued there,
The mother's love that I did see –
Last night put somber thoughts in me.

Though words somehow elude my mind –
My thought to holy events did bind,
And I prayed that Angela and Bill –
The Grace of God their heart would fill.

Now I take this time to honor you –
Those things as mother you did do,
Things that were so good and right –
Making possible that blessed night.

Epiphany – oh night select –
The good in life did well reflect,
These were the thoughts I would have read –
And I write them now – to you instead.

01-06/07-1995

This next is a FAX sent to my Rotary Club President. Dear
Wayne - On the computer with a little time on my hands so
thought I'd give you my thoughts (again) on club matters.

Rigolleto

How fortunate I was last night –
to share Rigolleto with you,
It gave to me such great delight –
my Spirit did renew.

As thrill of opera I did share –
I found my mind was caught,
Along with people sitting there –
in deep and other thought.

The Verdi opera most profound –
on emotions did engage,
And all the people that surround –
enforced what on the stage.

Verdi's opera takes great voice –
and orchestra as well,
Vibrant hall with settings choice –
this tragic opera tell.

All elements are then entwined –
for the opera to proceed,
Together skillfully refined –
if performance to succeed.

This poem I now do send to you –
on how this does relate,
To what our club is trying to do –
on our meeting, dining fate.

In a University atmosphere –
there should be little doubt,
It is quite plain and very clear –
that's what our name's about.

I hope that when we meet next week –
in the University location,
That will become the place we seek –
for many, not one – invocation.

01-12-1995

There was a member in my Sunday School Faith Class who I
had fairly close communications with. He was an outstanding
teacher who set a great example of how life was meant to be
lived and expressed. The next few poems came from his energy.

Loyalty

On Sunday as in class you spoke –
So many thoughts did you provoke –
The Book of Virtues you promote –
Your basic goodness did connote.

The Master Teacher that you are –
Puts you with Bennett on a par –
I respect the probing way you teach –
The deeper insights that you reach.

I made a pledge at start of year –
The mouth to close, the lesson hear –
The teacher's thought not interrupt –
Thus the thrust of lesson not disrupt.

To some degree today I failed –
As lesson on my mind prevailed –
Though in the main I did agree –
You provoked my thoughts on loyalty.

I felt a need these thoughts express –
So from my pledge did I digress –
To voice frustration in which caught –
On loyalty – to give my thought.

The dictionary makes quite plain –
As loyalty it does explain –
Allegiance, ardor, obligation –
Fidelity, devotion, association.

Yes loyalty all that combined –
With the best of virtues is entwined –
Its weight on everyone does fall –
As the good in each, in each does call.

And so today I found it strange –
That some thought loyalty could change –
That circumstance somehow dictates –
How loyalty to change relates.

Now change is with us constantly –
But firm and unchanging is loyalty –
To the best of virtues it compared –
Thus loyalty from change is spared.

Yes virtue, honor, loyalty –
Are changeless, timeless needs to me –
The keys to all that makes us good –
And I think by some misunderstood.

Since life is never ending change –
Then loyalty has need to range,
Though rearranged, complete and whole –
As a guiding force --- within the soul.

01-22-1995

Gus -- This came after Myrtle's critique of my thoughts on
"Loyalty". So more thoughts on loyalty that I hope helps clarify.

I Learn

The trees for the forest I could not see –
Till my wife explained it all to me –
For loyalty as she described –
Can surly change ---- can't be denied.

But loyalty by me explained –
Is constant, changeless, unrestrained –
I guess it's really play on word –
Depending how to one it's heard.

Loyalty does not dictate –
Compliance in a static state –
To thine own self must one be true –
And that's what I'm referring too.

Yes there are times it may require –
Actions far from one's desire –
Actions that may contradict –
What loyalty meant to depict.

That alters not, no not to me –
The depth and force of loyalty –
It will remain whole and complete –
Though may appear it in defeat.

The highest virtue – I believe –
Is loyalty – as I perceive –
Yes loyalty, that has been earned –
Comes from the soul, as I have learned.

But I have said all this before –
So there's no need to say much more –
To clearer expression I must return –
As from my wife – I learn – I learn.

01-22-1995

Gus – As you might expect – thoughts in the Loyalty poem were on my mind in class along with those below. I get frustrated, at times, because I am unable to express my inner thoughts without getting involved with something I have great difficulty talking about. The poem below is an effort to myself to try to at least get into perspective some of my frustration. Gus you are a superb teacher and wonderful person. I give Joyce the credit for that.

I Give

From experience this comes to me –
From exploits in my history –
As past events I have reviewed –
My respect for loyalty renewed.

From some past actions was distressed –
When from loyalty I thought digressed –
But since I've put it into place –
As the truth of loyalty I trace.

True loyalty can never change –
But priorities may rearrange –
Though by actions I've been pained –
My loyalty was unrestrained.

Loyalty needs are rearranged –
By events in life abruptly changed –
Conflicting loyalties that meet –
Diminish neither – both complete.

My life as then – I now would give –
For those who died to make them live –
But then, as now, I know – I know –
Not up to me, cannot be so.

I've run that past within my mind –
And prayer alone helps me to find –
That time in life that I resolved –
Loyalty code was deep involved.

I did the best – the best I could –
And with time's help now understood –
That past I cannot change – relive –
To God who knows – I give – I give.

01-22-1995

This next is another FAX to the Rotary Club president on our
topic at the time of moving.

Priority

Although car parking not the best –
The University setting met the test –
The Club agenda was fulfilled –
As the Rotary Spirit was instilled.

I know that the Club by people made –
Their talent, input, dues they paid –
Of course they really are the core –
Those members who come through the door.

But that door through which they walk –
For their fellowship and talk –
Must be door that's in a place –
That convention of Club will grace.

A place that meets their need –
Where the goals of Club succeed –
Where the environment won't distract –
And the members can interact.

A place that will compliment –
Our Rotary Club's intent –
A place befitting the name –
A reason that some members came.

The place where we met last week –
May be this place that we seek –
It seemed to have the essentials –
To enhance the Club credentials.

On this subject though said enough –
So this is the last of this stuff –
On wherever the place we agree –
The members have priority with me.

01-24-1995

A local Radio Station, KLBJ, was sponsoring a competition for
Valentine entries to the station. The winner would win flowers
to be delivered where they wanted them to be sent. I submitted,
via FAX, the following poem that DID win the flowers I had
delivered to my wife's Special Ed class room.

Valentine

In this radio age that we live –
I compete with others to give –
My thoughts on a special day –
In a unique and expressive way.

By using high tech to the max –
Computer and then of course FAX –
My love all Austin will know –
When this read on Ed Sossen's show.

But if somehow this not read –
And Ed chooses another instead –
I know what will always be mine –
Your true love – please be my --- Valentine.

All my love –

02-02-1995

Though that last poem won the contest, I along with it sent him the valentine poem I wrote to my wife the previous year along with the note: Ed, I like your humor in the morning and thought you might enjoy the poem I wrote my wife about this time last year. I've just sent you my entry to your? Valentine contest and send this for your amusement.

Then as the contest continued, they also asked for something with 30 words or less that made me come up with the following -

Again

Darling Myrtle – HON ! – Valentine flowers won –
Wouldn't it be nice – winning flowers twice.
In 30 words or less – Love Guy to impress –
You are always mine – My DARLING – Valentine!!

02-09-1995

My wife and I went to San Antonio to see the Musical Phantom of the Opera. As everyone knows, it is a very moving and powerful production. As the musical proceeded I was moved by the music. For some reason my mind changed much of what I was listening to. In the following few days I put those thoughts into the following words to the music.

If I Could Sing To You

If I could sing to you – what's in my heart,
The song would never end – if it should start,
The joy you give to me – would fill the air –
And all the love you bring into my life – would you find there.

If I could sing to you – this song of love,
With that of angel voice – from up above,
The words of song would show – what's deep in me –
The sound of song and music I now hear – love's symphony.

If I could sing to you – through song reveal,
All that you mean to me – the way I feel,
You are my everything – my world control –
With you and you alone am I complete – you make me whole.

If I could sing to you – with song rejoice,
The warmth of your embrace – your touch, your voice,
This I would pledge to you – to you my wife –
That you will ever, ever, ever be – my love for life.

If I could sing to you – expose the song,
Could I unmask, uncloak – emotions strong,
No greater song would be – on earth to find –
Than this, the Phantom song I sing to you --- within my mind.

03-04/05/06/07-1995

San Antonio (Phantom of the Opera)
Continental flights Austin to Houston to St. Louis
St. Louis Holiday Inn, Airport North

One of the families I flew for, had a strong interest in flying to
Hot Springs, Arkansas on a fairly frequent basis. Consequently
I would go to the well known Oaklawn Track often. My wife
and I would bet mainly on what looked good to us, such as color
or name of horse, or some other attribute other than the history
of the horse or rider involved. Using that method, we would
usually wind up in the plus category. One day however, after
being more educated by those around us as to what we should be
calculating, ie; the history and reputation of the horse and
jockey, our betting procedure changed, as well as our winning.

This next poem is a reflection of that.

Long Shot

Hot Springs, Arkansas – again I'm back,
At the Majestic Hotel – then to Oaklawn track,
There with others – to have some fun,
To play the horses – watch them run.

Before the horses – reach the gate,
With their statistics – I'll relate,
Whose the trainer – whose the jock,
How each horse stacks – against the clock.

See how others – their horse scored,
Check odds changing – on the board,
With all that data – then in place,
Go to the window – bet the race.

With the ticket – then in hand,
Make way back – to seat in stand,
From there to hear – they're at the gate,
The start of race – to then await.

They're off, they're off – away they go,
To see which beast – will win, place, show,
Which horse on track – which noble steed,
At the finish line – will be in lead.

The horse that's now – in front of pack,
May at race end – be in the back,
So not till finish line – they cross,
Can I compute – a win or loss.

When race is over – said and done,
The board will show – who lost, who won,
But photo finish – may delay,
How much the winning – tickets pay.

Ah yes it's fun – to pick and choose,
But ain't much fun – to mostly lose,
The horses on the track – that run,
It seems to me – have all the fun.

Back to the Majestic – I'll return,
And seems as if – I'll never learn,
That all the help – and stats I got,
Exclude the winner – you know --- the long shot!!!

03-17/18-1995
Hot Springs, Arkansas - Oaklawn Track/Majestic Hotel

Key

On this gold chain there is a key –
A token from my heart,
A token from inside of me –
My feelings to impart.

It seems each year about this time –
I search and search to find,
Befitting gift and lyric rhyme –
To show what's on my mind.

That on your birthday I renew –
And in my way reveal,
The joy that only comes from you –
The gift of love I feel.

This token key on chain of gold –
Portrays my love from start,
A key that only you do hold –
The entry ---- to my heart.

Happy Birthday Honey!!!!

03-24-1995

I hadn't received any recent e-mail correspondence from youngest daughter and her husband who live in Seattle. I always enjoyed what I received from them so to pull their chain a little, I wrote and e-mailed to them the following.

Seattle

You two up in Seattle –
I thought your cage I'd rattle –
In hopes to hear what's new –
And going on with you.

Because I haven't heard –
From CompuServe a word –
I thought I'd tweak your nose –
By sending you some prose.

Now prose I know this not –
But it's the best I got –
To tell you that I'm mad –
No message from you had.

So with CompuServe E-mail –
Your computer I'll assail –
Till you're back upon the net –
And some news from you I get.

My English ain't too good –
But I hope I'm understood –
There is more from whence this came –
So COMMUNICATE --- or take the blame!!!

03-29-1995

I found myself again at the Majestic Hotel in Hot Springs, Ark. with time on my hands. The following few entries came from that time period of my life.

To Be Or Not To Be

In a Shakespeare famed soliloquy –
He asks --- to be, or not to be,
He measures life with evils shown –
Against the fear of the unknown.

Could we but see beyond this place –
Behind the veil to ethereal space,
To see what dreams in death unfold –
What in that state to grasp, to hold.

If were revealed that mystery –
What follows death somehow could see,
This life we know would surely change –
Our thoughts and actions rearrange.

Those now in stress from life of care –
Might quickly, quickly hasten there,
The after death, the dream they see –
May be the dream to set them free.

Still others may be quite surprised –
To find their faith not realized,
By sleep of death, by dream deceived –
Opposed to all that they believed.

So the afterlife where we might go –
May well be one best not to know,
May be a dream when life we lose –
That had we known, we'd never choose.

We'd never choose no choice, just must –
Where there no need for faith or trust,
That all we treasure, love, hold dear –
May now be something but to fear.

So it is clear and plain to me –
On the question of to be or not to be,
All course of actions will turn awry –
If life, "to be", we defeat, deny.

For all, yes all, we see or seem –
To live, to die, to sleep, to dream,
Are Creation's dynamics, as one combined –
Life, death, sleep, dream, by God designed.

Only a fool would say not so –
Who thinks by chance through life we go,
To whom the Creator remains unknown –
And believes in only that which shown.

When all in life not to rejoice –
Then "not to be" to some a choice,
But to those who God in life do see –
The choice is life – yes life --- "To Be"!!

03-31-1995

Once again in and from Hot Springs

Oaklawn

Here I am at Oaklawn Track –
Flying and horses brought me back,
In a box by the finish line I sit –
In hope the odds to now outwit.

I know the chances are quite small –
Unless good luck on me does fall,
The odds of winning the Classix –
Like being hit with a ton of bricks.

But all the beauty that found here –
The sound of bugle crisp and clear,
Is focus that my mind does choose –
Not whether I will win or lose.

The first race over, course I lost –
Though wasn't much in dollar cost,
On first two bets it gave me trouble –
Since it was tied to Daily Double.

Oh well today I won't stay long –
My racing instincts aren't too strong,
On second race to win, place, show –
I've bet on two and then I'll go.

Whoops the second race I won –
So I'll stay longer – this is fun,
It's fun to watch your horse come in –
It's fun, it's fun – to win, win, win.

Race number three, the Classix start –
I'll bet this race before I part,
Since number two on Classix scored –
I'll bet that horse across the board.

The third race over and by a nose –
The horse that one not one I chose,
For most of race two held the lead –
But the winning horse another steed.

Those in the box, like me surprised –
The winner not horse they surmised,
Except for one who beat the odds –
A lady I'm sure cavorts with Gods.

From the box on finish line I'll go –
Collect my meager place and show,
Since my Classix now said and done –
I'll leave before fourth race begun.

Leave the friends who box did share –
Oaklawn track in their good care,
Scotts', the Winters', Rauschers' too –
It was fun to share Oaklawn -- with you.

04-01-1995

Respect

Two families who I'm flying for –
the Butlers' and the Scotts',
They typify the difference tween –
the haves and the have nots.

By haves I'm not referring to –
the measure of their wealth,
But rather to the status of –
their grace and social health.

I've known them now for many years -
in a bond that has no measure,
The family, friends they share with me –
are relationships I treasure.

It's not the job or hope of gain –
why thoughts I'm now revealing,
But warmth of friendship on my mind –
that engenders this good feeling.

I know all things must come to end –
for time is fickle, fleeting,
But time now offers me this chance –
to express my heartfelt greeting.

To express while now I have the time –
as our lives are rearranging,
I want to tell them they have earned –
my respect that remains --- unchanging.

04-01-1995

P.S.

This day I see is April First –
a day known for leg pulling,
But the above is far from that –
is a pull from heart fulfilling.

This note followed the next poem there at the Majestic:

Wasn't sleeping well. A refrain I had heard days earlier kept
running through my mind. Something to words of – "In my
Gondola". I thought it was beautiful music and put my words to
it. I won't say anything about dreams I was having. Anyway, I
sang the words to the music to my tape recorder, went back to
bed and fell asleep.

Our Song

There's a song – that I hear tonight –
Song of love – sweet refrain,
From the past – what I hear tonight –
Is the music – that leads me – to wander –
Down memory lane.

And my heart – nearly bursts with joy –
As the song – fills my mind,
Fills my mind – with the thought of you –
The love and – the passion – the life we –Together find.

Take my hand – feel the song in me –
Song of love – ours alone,
Take my hand – and you'll hear with me –
The beauty – enchantment – the magic –
Your love has shown.

Ah my love – could I sing tonight –
This sweet strain – clear and strong,
All the world – would be captured by –
The awe and – the wonder – the rapture –
Of this --- our song.

04-02-1995 (3:30am)

What Was That???

When my life on earth is over –
And is totaled up the score,
As I'm laid beneath the clover –
To roam this place no more.

As my mind to new form binding –
And flame of life snuffed out,
I will gasp at that unwinding –
"What the hell was that all about?!".

04-05-1995

Hot Tip

I wasn't going out to the track –
From horses I'd take a break,
Today I thought I would cut some slack –
A breather from Oaklawn would take.

I thought instead I would spend the day –
In the National Park that is here,
To wander the trails that make their way –
Around West Mountain that's near.

But first to the airport I had to go –
Some things on our airplane to check,
And there was no way for me then to know –
That the visit all my plans would wreck.

For there at the airport my mind was changed –
By the power of spoken word,
My plans for the day were all rearranged –
By a conversation out there that I heard.

A tip from that conversation I got –
From people who seemed in the know,
On a horse in the sixth, a tip so red hot –
That in haste to the track had to go.

At Oaklawn the race had yet to begin –
To a ticket on four I did get,
I went with that horse cross the board to win –
On that red hot tip I did bet.

Friends at the track with me graciously share –
Their box to enjoy the race,
By the finish line and with them then from there –
To see how the horses would place.

Four really looked great and started quite fast –
Kept pace up front with the lead,
But then you might know as the finish line past –
He was far from the winning steed.

The race then now over a new change in thought –
No longer did track interest me,
The glow of day to my senses now brought –
An urge from Oaklawn to be free.

And so from the box from Oaklawn did depart –
To the beauty outside did return,
Where from there in my mind this poem did start –
To project what from day I did learn.

Was it a tip on a horse that my plans rearranged –
That kept me from a mountain to roam?
Or was it by will that this day for me changed –
To give me an excuse for this poem?

But I need no excuse for a poem to write –
For my feelings on life to extol,
So I guess then this day with all its delight –
That hot tip on a horse --- did control!

04-14-1995

Grady's Grill

I find myself in Grady's Grill –
The needs of appetite to fill,
And upon the menu there to see –
Are choices that appeal to me.

I will not make a choice in haste –
I want a meal to please my taste,
I want a meal to match what's here –
This pleasant, Majestic atmosphere.

Within a glass front grill discern –
Plump chickens that before me turn,
Chickens slowly browning, sweet –
A choice on menu hard to beat.

There's steak and fish, pasta too –
Upon the menu there to view,
The entrée choice is hard to make –
With meals they fry or broil, bake.

But well I know I cannot lose –
With the menu item I may choose,
For Grady's only serves the best –
To any palate meets the test.

So Majestic Hotel my venerable host –
To your Grady's Grill I drink a toast,
To the Chef and staff that make it go –
I raise a glass – to the best that I know.

04-15-1995

I was still at the Majestic Hotel when the Murrah Federal
Building in Oklahoma City was bombed by Timothy McVeigh.
This next poem is something I wrote then ----

Embrace

In Oklahoma what we saw –
Was a ruthless, callous breach of law –
An evil, senseless tragedy –
That will live forever in memory.

A cruel and brutal, ugly crime –
A transgression unequaled in our time –
Where murdering cowards with intent –
Killed babies, infants – innocent.

Inside my heart I weep, I weep –
With silent tears that there I keep –
This horrendous act so inhumane –
Has reawakened all my pain.

Oh it's hard for me to see –
How this event could ever be –
Who would by choice, by their own will –
These innocents to maim and kill.

There is no cause can justify –
The innocent, full life deny –
Whoever did this horrible deed –
Their wicked goal, must not succeed.

Their act of terror we must beat –
Or our way of life is in defeat –
Although these things not understood –
From every evil must come good.

The good must come to make us whole –
To give us peace within our soul –
But terrorists we first must find –
To put this ache, this pain behind.

Their punishment, be swift and sure –
Their place in hell for them secure –
And with that thought to find relief –
From this our sorrow, shock, our grief.

Now for the living I will pray –
That in their sadness on this day –
God showers them with Holy Grace –
As He holds their loved ones – in – embrace.

04-20/21-1995

This next was written as an explanation to one of the wonderful
ladies that I was a personal and corporate pilot for.

Wine

I am sorry Mrs. Scott – the wine in Austin forgot,
And I accept the blame – to Hot Springs without it we came.
Of course I feel quite bad – for lots of room we had,
The airplane load was light – so the time to do it right.

The fault alone is mine – that we came without the wine,
I hope it's not too late – the following thoughts to state.
I know that I failed to do – request that was tasked by you,
Now as you might surmise – with rhyme – I apologize.

Please accept my apology – with the miniature here you see,
As a token of my regret – for the wine I did surely forget.
This miniature bottle of wine – does crux of the problem define,
I found it at Tillman's today – out of sight --- and not on display.

04-21-1995

This next was another report made to that lady I flew for.

Mrs. Scott: Here is the report you asked for on our visit to
Branson. Rik and I didn't stay long in town, but both agreed it
is clean, pretty and very commercial. We had a delightful
dinner at a café and left before dark.

Branson Report

Point Lookout, Clark

Just outside of Branson, Mo –
An airport on the map does show,
With a runway short upon a hill –
That puts to test a pilot's skill.

On a hill in the Ozarks it's atop –
At either end there is a drop,
At neither end is an overrun –
So operations here may not be fun.

For smaller airplanes should be ok –
With lots of room for them to play,
But larger aircraft should think twice –
For them the hazards not so nice.

If weather's great and wind just right –
The airport may not be too tight,
But still if choice were up to me –
Another airport we would see.

To Harrison, Ark we'd probably go –
Or Springfield Regional at Springfield Mo,
A forty minute drive from either one –
Bit scenery's terrific before drive done.

Though by thirty minutes does drive extend –
With this report to you I send,
That all things considered I have to voice –
Point Lookout, Clark ---- is not good choice.

04-27-1995
Harrison, Ark
Comfort Inn

Another follows with grandchildren motivational input.

Discovery Zone

I sit in this place at a table alone,
This neat place for children, Discovery Zone,
Where here in frolic they run and play,
To share with each other joy of this day.

The Looney tune music within this place,
The happy smile upon their face,
Their joyous screams and shouts of glee,
All have a great affect on me.

Embraced within this atmosphere,
Are my children's children playing here,
I watch them running all around,
To the fun, fun things that here abound.

From them great patience I am taught,
As in travails of play they're caught,
I know that they expect from me,
The cure to imagined slights they see.

These wonderful children, gifts of life,
I attribute to Myrtle, our honoree, my wife,
For she's the one as you all know,
Whose energy makes good things to grow.

Now I started this to pass some time,
To put my harried thoughts to rhyme,
And what I found here as I sat alone,
Was a tribute to life at Discovery Zone.

To a mother, grandmother, my best friend,
Who only the best in herself does extend,
This teacher of children, great lady with class,
Let us all in her honor – drink a toast – raise a glass!!!

05-13-1995

The next two written with my daughter in mind.

Myrtle E

To my daughter Myrtle E – This check that comes from we –
The we – your mother and I – We send for you to fly.
We'd send another check too – If guy who's married to you –
Would make the trip more right – By joining you in flight.

My English ain't too good – So hope it's understood –
We miss an awful lot – Youngest daughter we got.
We want to see real bad – Baby daughter we had –
And with this we now beseech – Hope to see you on the beach.

05-26-1995

Master Plan

There are no words can justly state –
No song or poem that can relate,
The thoughts this evening on my mind –
Of a precious daughter that I find.

My love for her this night did start –
A flood of warmth in mind and heart,
For this dear child I seldom see –
Because she lives so far from me.

I know not why these thoughts began –
The words in mind come not from plan,
But from emotions that I feel –
That on this page I now reveal.

I wish that God her life does bless –
With joy and peace and happiness,
Much as the joy I feel this night –
From thoughts of her that give delight.

Although I miss that she's not here –
I know in mind she's always near,
I am so blessed to know that she –
Forever will my daughter be.

I feel a need to share my thought –
This depth of love to me now brought,
A love will last till end of time –
A father's love here put to rhyme.

I hope to her my thoughts do reach –
And that this summer on the beach,
She and her husband both will share –
The beauty of their presence there.

Now if they do these thoughts in me –
I know with purpose had to be,
And that this poem I began –
From an unknown source – a Master Plan.

05-27-1995

The next were thoughts on a Sunday School Fellowship lesson
led by a great Class leader, Gus Stewart.

Quail

I saw an itty bitty quail –
And sprinkled salt upon its tail –
Then made of it a tasty treat –
Upon my table there to eat.

It came to me this silly thought –
Before Gus lesson to us taught –
Bev Waddle told of tiny quail –
That on her senses did prevail.

She told of quail that she did see –
That filled her heart with empathy –
She wanted someone who would care –
With tiny bird their love to share.

Unlike Bev's, my thoughts ran –
More to a culinary plan –
To me that bird would make a hit –
While turning slowly on a spit.

On fate of quail we didn't dwell –
For quail with Bev was doing well –
So since there was no urgent need –
Into the lesson we proceed.

Now Gus was teacher impromptu –
He taught as only he could do –
His finer insights with us share –
As we said together childhood prayer.

The lesson pulled from out the mind –
The inner thoughts in each to find –
The varied thoughts of everyone –
We heard before the lesson done.

From what in lesson I did learn –
My thoughts o tiny quail return –
It seemed a great dichotomy –
The thoughts in Bev to those in me.

To Bev the quail was birdie sweet –
To me a tidbit one might eat –
The differences are quite profound –
But truth in either concept found.

So Gus again with perception clear –
Life's understanding brings more near –
All my guttural senses he assail –
To never again devour a little quail.

05-28-1995

Thoughts in this next, are on a great sermon given by a member
of our congregation.

Blessed

A member in the church today –
preached a sermon strong,
Gave message that was quite superb –
but ah – a trifle long.

He preached as only he can do –
what he's seen and heard,
In style of his did he relate –
with wise and vibrant word.

So good it was to hear him speak –
life's stage to analyze,
With wit and clarity to tell –
what on the stage to prize.

A little girl with father's hand –
the happiness seen there,
An aged lady in a world of art –
her feelings in silence share.

The airborne show in garden seen –
questioned by his wife,
Analyzed and explained by him –
as love that fosters life.

These life events did he compare –
to the Beatitudes just read,
Where blessed within the passage read –
as happy now instead.

Happy to him was a better word –
and he used it well of course,
Still as his sermon neared its close –
was blessed held greater force.

For I was happy with his words –
his preaching that was clear,
But blessed indeed when ending came –
for was a little long – I fear.

06-04-1995

Thoughts looking out the window on a sunny, windy, cloudy day
in Falfurrias, Texas.

Hold Dear

This sphere I find myself upon – that travels on in space,
This ever spinning planet earth – that round the sun does race,
Is my home within the Universe – the only place I know,
Where needs to nourish body life – my Creator did bestow.

Survival needs that foster growth – there's water, food and air,
There's shelter from the elements – there largess everywhere,
I use these gifts for well I must – the breadth of them apply,
Sustaining life here given to me – for reasons I know not why.

I know not why all this was made – this Universe Creation,
Why is there life on planet earth – what is the God relation?
Was there a purpose all this made – a plan of God my Maker?
Why given to me a zest for life – as both giver and a taker?

So I try to do the best I can – with the life that is given to me,
To use the gifts that to me relate – all my energies to free,
To show to people that I love – who on my life will impact,
That I feel a power I can't explain – and with it interact.

I know there's pain and suffering – sin and evil all around,
Sickness and death, disaster – grief and sorrow still abound,
But the hand of a Mighty Creator – all this for reason design,
And my time upon this planet – to this moment did now assign.

So with reverence of this my calling – respect for life I feel,
In great awe of this my Creation – depth of my thoughts reveal,
To express emotions within me – to Force I feel ever so near,
Mysterious power almighty – give thanks for life – I hold dear.

06-10-1995

I had written in an earlier poem titled "Wine", that I had
forgotten to bring the wine from Austin to Hot Springs for the
fiftieth wedding anniversary of a wonderful couple I flew for.
This next poem finishes that particular episode.

Fine Wine

The wine to Hot Springs I finally got,
And not just a little but really a lot,
Ten cases were flown here to be exact,
Eight white two red and that's a fact.

From Capitol Beverage where it was hoard,
In a far off corner where beer also stored,
Moved into my wagon fit snuggly inside,
Then out to the airport unbroken to ride.

When out there ten cases lifted once more,
From Mercury to Merlin to properly store,
Front to the back deftly balanced the load,
Then Mueller to Memorial securely they rode.

Take-off to landing flight they did make,
Went ever so smoothly no bottle did break,
But hazards not over for journey not done,
From airport to Arlington their final run.

Mrs. Scott with a pen labeled each case,
As into the Cadillac the wine I did place,
From warehouse wagon to airplane now car,
Some wine I'd forgotten has really come far.

On to the Arlington in class they did drive,
In parking garage at the hotel to arrive,
Ten cases of white and red wine taken there,
Were finally given to the manager's care.

Wine that now coming to end of its fate,
Home in the Arlington near its final state,
Is wine to be used in a grand celebration,
To honor achievement of a lengthy relation.

As the saga of wine now comes nearly to end,
For wine once forgotten the following extend,
No need for a miniature with this odyssey,
Heavy lifting of wine is the token from me.

Fine wine to be raised in a toast to a pair,
Who for fifty good years a marriage did share,
To Morin Scott and to Joy his wonderful wife,
A toast in their honor the gold in their life.

Happy fiftieth anniversary!!!

06-13-1995
Hot Springs, Ark (Majestic Hotel)

This next brief note was as well related to the above poem. It was written to the daughter of the wonderful lady referenced.

Dear SuSu,

I wrote the enclosed poem shortly after we spoke. It came easily for I have only the highest respect and love for your parents. I hope it is suitable for you to use and thank you for the opportunity.

Fiftieth

For you by SuSu your friends tasked –
a favorite memory to share,
A photograph, story or anecdote asked –
from people who love you and care.

For fifty years your lives have been –
very happily joined as one,
So I hope this poem I now begin –
pays you tribute before it is done.

To you to express was a privilege for me –
your airplane, your Merlin to fly,
It not only was fun but an honor to be –
your Captain there up in the sky.

Now fifty years is a whole lot of time –
to amass both the good and the bad,
Thrust of it all won't fit into this rhyme –
and for that I am sure you are glad.

For there may be tales funny, risqué –
you wouldn't want some folks to hear,
But I with thoughts of my own now will play –
to construct what in poem will appear.

The words that I write, the feelings in me –
will determine what outcome will show,
So only good thoughts of you will you see –
of you both there's naught bad that I know.

The best of remembrance of you have I got –
in my heart you are in a warm place,
To me you are great and I cherish a lot –
your family, your friends and your grace.

Now all who read this I well know for sure –
this knowledge of you also share,
That like me in your presence they are secure –
with the goodness and beauty found there.

So dear Joy and dear Morin – Mr. & Mrs. Scott –
with fondness to you this is sent,
From family and friends who sure love you alot –
the fifty y ears that you represent.
Fifty years close together as man and wife –
what you both with your values believe,
Represents to us all the true essence of life –
what two people with love – can achieve.

06-20/21-1995
Austin/Bay City

This next was a FAX that I had sent to our local radio station on
another competition they were sponsoring concerning
patriotism. It contained the following Note: I will be leaving
Austin in the morning around 8:00am and won't be back till
Sunday evening. The above is also to music which sounds pretty
good. At least to me. That FAX number also has a answering
machine gadget with it. I don't expect to win anything but
thought you might like this approach. Thanx for the flowers to
my wife over Valentine's Day. Sincerely ----

I Love America Because

I love America because –
America is home to me.

I love America because –
Here live my friends my family.

I love America because –
Of beauty in her that I see.

I love America because –
She's land of opportunity.

I love America because –
Her people strive for harmony.

I love America because –
She sets my soul and Spirit free.

I love America because –
In Her I hear a symphony -----

Giving her love - her love to me.

06-21-1995

What follows was something I wrote while attending a wedding
that my wife and I were invited to. The wedding was for a
relative on my wife's side of the family. The marriage was a
festive and meaningful event.

Celebrate

Were here tonight to celebrate,
With Frank and Bobby to relate,
To offer them right from the start,
Best wishes that come from the heart.

Tomorrow their new life will begin,
With relationship they enter in,
Their love together now to share,
With all the goodness they find there.

When they are joined as man and wife,
Their future offers joyous life,
With holy bonds of marriage tight,
Their days together fun and bright.

Her children standing by her side,
Bobby will be "blushing" bride,
And Frank of course with his kids too,
Before us all will say "I do".

From many States did we all come,
From New York, Florida – Texas some,
To witness this, this grand event,
Before on honeymoon they're sent.

When to Wyoming they finally go,
No wild oats will either sow,
For on their honeymoon will be,
Granddaughters with them there you see.

Now our imagination it does pique,
This union that is quite unique,
So our good fortune tonight to thank,
In a toast with love – to Bobby and Frank.

CHEERS!!!

06-23-1995
Bastrop, La (Bastrop Inn)

This next continues my thought process during that time period
in Bastrop, La.

Presence

Again I'm in the presence of –
The family of the gal I love –
Where she was born, Bastrop, L A –
To share her cousin's wedding day.

With relatives on her dad's side –
Who here in Bastrop do reside –
Bobby Coats and her children too –
The history of the Coats review.

To burial ground the girls did go –
To honor those at peace they know –
The Coats' and Leavells' buried there –
Who common ground in Bastrop share.

Today to Mer Rouge we will go –
To watch in church a wedding show –
But yesterday we poked around –
To see what from the past we found.

First day to Bobbie's house we went –
We used directions that she sent –
With them we drove around and round –
Until her house we finally found.

Bobbie's directions though direct –
Had too many check points she select –
Just seven miles from Bastrop Inn –
But in Mer Rouge our miles begin.

For cows, the dairy, home, Red hill –
We looked and looked that is until –
All roads around Mer Rouge exhaust –
Before conceding we were lost.

Then for her address we did look –
An lo and behold that tactic took –
For her house was easy there to see –
Exactly where it ought to be.

Again next day that game we played –
When back to the cemetery we strayed –
The loved ones girls had found before –
It seems somehow were there no more.

From morning when they first were here –
Two dear departed disappear –
No trace of them could now be found –
We feared they left this hallowed ground.

But earlier footsteps we did trace –
Until we found the proper the proper place –
Then most relieved we went our way –
To prepare for Bobbie's wedding day.

That afternoon with Bobbie and Frank –
In their good company wine we drank –
Then as it is with this family –
The talk soon of their history.

And so with that I've said enough –
I want not bore with all this stuff –
Bout Grandpa John his brothers and such –
I know that's really much – too much.

Back to Mer Rouge and reason we came –
To change a Coats to Wondrasch name –
To join with Frank and oh yes --- Bobbie –
In that pattern of life called ---- history.

That look in past they think profound –
This family really loves to expound –
And I have learned to patient be –
When I'm with my wife and – her family.

06-23/26-1995
Bastrop, La (Bastrop Inn) & Austin, Tx

The following was submitted to a Rotary friend of mine:

Terry –

This is what I started at your installation as President. If you can use it in any way please do. Take the liberty of changing it if you like. Let me know if there is anything I can do to assist you. As you know, I am not an organizer or leader but within my ability will do what I can.

Friend

To Wayne Hall our Rotarian friend –
The University Area Club does extend,
Our thanks for what you represent –
For your term as our president.

With vim and with vigor you lead –
So that all club endeavors succeed,
You were there with your intellect, wit –
In maintaining a club quite close knit.

To our roots by you we were brought –
With your energy to new home we sought,
To the place where club got its start –
The University of which we are part.

We look forward to joining you there –
The Rotarian ethic to share,
So our hand do we all now extend –
In a toast to you Wayne --- our dear friend.

Cheers to "OUR FRIEND IN ROTARY"
on this and "EVERY" day. !!!

06-29-1995

This next brings back a great memory of the time when my wife and I were visiting our daughter and family in Spring, Texas for 4th of July. The poem describes well the memory.

Fishing

With Gary fishing we did go –
To a Catfish farm that he did know –
We went there with this Macho man –
The eight of us in his green van.

Because they'd be a hungry bunch –
Gary packed the kids a lunch –
Then because he's awfully nice –
He stopped along the way for ice.

When to the farm we did arrive –
He bought some icky worms alive –
These nasty worms then Gary took –
And stuck them on a fishing hook.

Halie, Heather and Samantha too –
With Gary's help knew what to do –
Along with Linzee caught a fish –
Like AJ and KC got their wish.

Not just fish biting though –
Ants by the jillions there did grow –
Samantha and KC were so sweet –
Bit them on their hands and feet.

Those stupid ants at times we fought –
But four neat fish were finally caught –
Two lucky fish though got away –
With other fish in pond to play.

Well Heather got the biggest one –
But all the kids had loads of fun –
Until the fish were cut and clean –
And that they thought was really mean.

Back to the house with Macho man –
We drove again in Gary's van –
After that fishing lesson we got –
From a man who loves – his children – a lot.

07-01-1995
Spring, Tx

The following thoughts were of an aviator who passed on to God's care. I was honored by a dear friend, Marvin Ledyard, who asked if I had something I could share with him on this particular passing. I did not know Jayesh Dave, but I'm sure I would have liked him had I had the opportunity. I believe he shared my deep love for flying.

Divine

Jayesh Dave would flying go –
The wonders of flight to extend,
In joy of flight only pilots know –
Where the heart and the Spirit blend.

To master an airplane up in the sky –
With the freedom that it does instill,
Gives a closeness to God we can't deny –
The quest of His purpose fulfill.

Flight gives to us a comfort of mind –
A wholeness of life bringing peace,
Where nearer to God our serenity find –
From cares of the earth know release.

No stronger bond to God that we know –
Than tie that we feel when in flight,
So if while flying to God we should go –
The warmth of His love will be right.

Now Jayesh has gone into God's care –
In flight with God's purpose align,
In heaven soaring with us still to share –
Love of flying - from a Master – Divine !!

07-02-1995

Following a Sunday School class lesson given by a good friend, I
wrote something on the lesson and sent it to my friend. It began
to him with: Gus – As you might expect – Myrtle says I am
psychotic — somewhat.

Myths

The bible myths we tried sort out –
As some of them Gus talked about,
Which myth, what truth to disavow –
What would our faith accept, allow.

Those myths to us that he relate –
Found room within my mental state,
Absorbed and questioned by my mind –
With thoughts in bible that I find.

First myth to us that Gus impart –
Was how Creation had its start,
That on first day myth does instruct –
Heaven and earth did God construct.

At His command then came first light –
As all progressed was good and right,
Then pleased with time that He invest –
On the seventh day He took a rest.

To Gus the Sabbath not God's plan –
But a structure of religious man,
To justify what was practiced then –
So would be continued again and again.

Now with that premise can agree –
Because it makes some sense to me,
Since God through man the bible wrote –
Then myth does thought of man connote.

In searching still for God's intent –
From there to other myths Gus went,
With the Will of God comparison make –
To Adam and Eve and the venomous snake.

Gus with skill the class did lead –
And we his expert knowledge heed,
Still when the thrust of lesson done –
My thoughts on God where first begun.

With what God is I remain unsure –
But with Creation I am most secure,
The existence of God no myth to me –
But a function of logic – a --- certainty.

07-09-1995

Inverter

I find myself again tonight –
Aboard a crowded Southwest flight –
From El Paso now to close a day –
That started in a hectic way.

Last night on flight from Arlington –
Was really when this day begun –
Near time of midnight flying high –
Number two inverter decided to die.

The night was dark but weather good –
And the failure symptoms understood –
So when number one switched on the line –
The flight continued smooth and fine.

Six passengers in back knew naught –
Thus had no need to be distraught –
With landing slick and flight then done –
The compliments from all was won.

Was now past midnight much too late –
For woes too maintenance to relate –
I thought for sure that I could find –
In the morning inverter of proper kind.

This morning early to Georgetown Jet –
I flew the Merlin for inverter to get –
Inverter was changed according to plan –
And that is when my heartburn began.

Flight to Ruidoso was to leave at twelve –
As into the guts of the airplane we delve –
To try to find that cantankerous part –
That was causing inverter not to start.

Now Georgetown Jet had a workload high –
But with my urgings they comply –
Gary probed and tested all around –
And with expertise a bad solenoid found.

Lucky we were that a new one they had –
To replace in the circuit solenoid bad –
With circuit restored I hit the switch –
And inverter responded without a hitch.

Then back to Austin I hurriedly flew –
The Ruidoso timetable to there renew –
Since Georgetown Jet had saved the day –
Just three hours late we were on our way.

In flight to Ruidoso I finally relaxed –
I put into low gear a system overtaxed –
Was Eddie and Renee, their beautiful smile –
Put it into perspective and made it worthwhile.

So here I am back to Austin in flight –
Thoughts of the day in my mind to write –
For a Merlin Three I'm a hired nursemaid –
To continue safe flying for which I am paid.

07-12-1995
Written on Southwest flight from El Paso to Austin

More family memories.

Family Fun

Again I went to Padre Isle –
To be with family for a while.
In Ninety-five the month of July –
To enjoy the sand, the surf, the sky.

Island House is where we meet –
To get the sand beneath our feet,
To feel the sun upon our face –
And enjoy the beauty of this place.

Each morning a gazebo shelter made –
To offer from the sun some shade,
To stake a claim upon the beach –
That was easy from the condo to reach.

Throughout the day then to and fro –
From Beach to pool the kids would go,
And they of course the agenda set –
What from the day adults would get.

That is to say except for me –
At times in room I watched TV,
The Senate hearings or trial of OJ –
Determined how I'd spend my day.

The week was fun, all went so great –
With fun and laughter we relate,
The love of family filled the air –
At Island House off Corpus there.

As I look back, on week reflect –
No special moment can select,
Each moment wove to join as one –
One perfect week of family fun.

07-23-1995

And once again in Hot Springs, Ark.

Flavor

The Majestic Hotel where now I sit –
To pass some time with word and wit,
In mood controlled by a mountain scene –
The hotel pool with blue water clean.

I'm looking down on kids at play –
Enjoying the pool, the sun, the day,
They reinforce this mood I'm in –
That caused this poem to begin.

Hot Springs Arkansas where all this at –
Amid terrain that's far from flat,
The mountain West and Mountain East –
Provide my mind with a bounteous feast.

Along with mountains that surround –
Rivers and lakes are close around,
This breadth of beauty oh so near –
Is the reason why I like it here.

The Majestic Hotel gives me the time –
To organize my thoughts to rhyme,
The flavor of this day to taste –
That flavor to record and not to waste.

So while the flavor does embrace –
My inner feelings I will trace,
The blush and aroma try to relate –
That Arkansas is a beautiful State.

PS:

To you ladies at this SPA Resort –
Who also in the pool cavort,
You are not the kids of which I spoke –
Although these thoughts you could provoke.

For the atmosphere you sensitize –
As in pool you do your exercise,
And it's really very clear to see –
You enjoy each other's – company.

08-01/02-1995
Hot Springs, Ark (Majestic Hotel)

Miscellaneous, extraneous thoughts continue to follow with a
note of explanation.

Not Poetry

I put my thoughts to rhyme a lot –
Still an Edgar Allen Poe I'm not,
And an Omar Khayyam I neither am –
To even compare would be a sham.

I lack the imagination to create –
Life that impacts me do I relate,
I reconstruct what there I feel –
Emotions in words I then reveal.

So I make no claim of creativity –
I have no need a great poet to be,
My writings just that, a mere diary –
Events in my life and not – poetry.

08-03-1995

I received compliments today on my, so called, poetry. I find
this flattering and yet somewhat unearned. I am no poet, for
poets write for others. I write only to satisfy myself and if in the
process others enjoy what I have written, then I am both happy
for them and also flattered that they related, in some way, to my
expression. I can't explain it but I'm sure I think more clearly
when I put things to rhyme. That makes of me NO POET!!! It
is something I can rarely turn on at will – it just seems to take
over and I follow along. My wife says that indicates I'm
psychotic.

Aren't we all???

P.S.

My wife I think would much prefer –
That poetry I would defer,
That it's an ego thing with me –
The writing of my poetry.

She thinks that I am too possessed –
With poetry my mind obsessed,
With her on that I do agree –
My life is wrapped in poetry.

On that I cannot be more plain –
It's poetry that keeps me sane,
Within its grasp I find release –
That gives my life – an inner peace.

08-04-1995

This next, Casa Caliche, was written prior to another visit to the
home of dear friends, Dr. Clift and Sue Price. It was to be our
Faith Class gathering at their beautiful home by Lake Travis.

Casa Caliche

Casa Caliche – in wooded expanse,
Life's Holy purpose does enhance,
Amid tranquil lakeside scenery,
Casa Caliche's charm embraces me.

Enfolds my mind with peaceful thought,
To witness here what God has wrought,
To see the workings of His hand,
How God did shape and form this land.

The depth of vistas, hue of sky,
All soothe the sense, please the eye,
They permeate the heart and soul,
To make the Spirit strong and whole.

Within this home and here around,
Are special bonds of friendship found,
A Holy gift from up above,
Reflections of a Father's love.

Yes the vibrancy of this atmosphere,
Gives evidence that God is near,
Of everything He is a part,
The mind and body, soul and heart.

As I contemplate and savor this,
I feel on cheek like angel kiss,
A soft lake breeze that says to me,
God's in His Heaven - at – Casa Caliche!

08-08-1995

This next continues more on the wine saga to the Majestic Hotel
in Hot Springs, Arkansas.

More Wine

Again with cases numbered nine –
To Hot Springs flew with wine, more wine,
Nine cases loaded in the nose –
There nestled snuggly to repose.

Wine, more wine put me to test –
To fit it in with all the rest,
Eight passengers their bags and such –
Was close to being much – too much.

I calculated to a "T" –
Stats I thought the load would be,
C.G. and weight came out alright –
But space it seems could be quite tight.

On Friday morning Roy and Ann –
Arrived with guests and most their clan,
Main plan was followed with no switch –
And all were loaded without hitch.

To keep the airplane in C.G. –
Tom Granger sat up front with me,
His cabin seat with bags I stack –
So there no room for him in back.

The airplane load was quite a sight –
As I maneuvered the aisle for flight,
It was a challenge to compete –
With those on couch to miss their feet.

Then all secure and take-off done –
With wine, more wine the flight begun,
The mood of all was light, relaxed –
And no one seems was over taxed.

Food tray in flight was passed around –
As I smooth air for journey found,
But during let down got our lumps –
As stormy clouds gave us some bumps.

With touchdown smooth upon concrete –
The flight from Austin was complete,
And this saga that here I now define –
Is a product of wine, yes wine – more wine.

08-25/26/27-1995
Hot Springs, Ark (Majestic Hotel)

Grandchildren's influence   again.

Exhilerama

We took granddaughters out one day –
To Exhilerama there to play –
Halie, Heather and Samantha B. –
Who remind us of our daughters three.

On Saturday morning we did all –
Find our way to Memorial Mall –
For forty minutes we did drive –
Before to Mall we did arrive.

When the Mall Exhilerama had to find –
Instruction of children I had to mind,
They insisted I follow directions clear –
And sure enough Exhilerama appear.

We parked the wagon and entered in –
Where all the fun and noise begin –
In Exhilerama's excitement then caught –
As our wrist bands from an agent bought.

First thing we did was take a ride –
In a circular cage we got inside –
The kids all thought it really great –
As for me I nearly regurgitate.

From there to other rides they went –
To a play scape where many hours spent –
My wife and I were near worn out –
In hearing children laugh and shout.

For lunch we left and made me glad –
Went into the Mall where pizza had –
But then returned we did to fray –
To all the noise and children's play.

When near exhausted we thought best –
To wander the Mall and maybe rest –
Where in the Mall for them was bought –
Porcelain clowns that their fancy caught.

From there we sought a movie to find –
But none did we see of children king –
So we left the Mall to homeward drive –
But first to a video store arrive.

There Oliver and Little Women we rent –
And then to the house we finally went –
Where Lasagna, pop corn and ice-cream ate –
Before Oliver was over was really late.

Reluctantly with all this done –
Bed time preparation was then begun –
But girls were good and listened well –
When eyes were closed to sleep they fell.

So Exhilerama's story now comes to end –
With our energy gone no more to expend –
T his day nearly over was really great –
Because with Grandchildren in fun --- we relate.

09-03-1995
Spring, Tx

BAD, BAD, BAD

Sometimes it makes Grandchildren glad –
When they drive their Grandpa mad, mad, mad,
It seems at times they scream and bawl –
To send their Grandpa up the wall.

I think it's in their evil brain –
They want to drive Grandpa insane,
And there is nothing he can say –
To make them change their devil way.

At Randall's store they shout and run –
I guess to them was really fun,
And I guess their gut it really please –
When like little pigs ate sample cheese.

They showed another side, a flaw –
When they told a tale about a straw,
Halie said that MiMi gave her OK –
For her with curly straw to play.

I fussed and fussed and said no more –
Would I ever take them to a store,
And threatened when the shopping done –
Never again would take them to have fun.

Well back at home all three did coax –
They knew the threats were only hoax –
Their energies made their Grandpa glad –
For these children were GRAND! – not bad, bad, bad.

09-03-1995
Spring, Tx

What follows is part of a FAX that I had sent to Liz Carpenter:

Intact

At Stafford's Meadow Farm Saturday –
Liz Carpenter with limerick did play –
Before her limerick was told –
Related ailments of old –
Then continued with limerick quite bold.

With her wit and her humor homespun –
Zeroed in on the groin for her fun –
In our mind she create -
That when there operate –
A doctor by chance might castrate.

She cautioned all doctors "DON'T BOTCH" –
When you fool with a body near crotch –
Yes the audience react –
When Liz end with a fact –
Warning Docs to leave all things – INTACT !!!

09-17-1995

Liz - It was nice seeing you Saturday. The limerick, as all you write, was humorous and to the point. Thank you for the laugh and good feelings.
The next two poems were the last that I wrote to the families I was a personal and corporate pilot for. I was approaching the age of 65 and the insurers of the aircraft were going to require that I fly with a copilot during charter operations when I reached that age. That was not a choice I was willing to make and decided it was time for retirement.

Last Report

The time has come for the last report –
On operational accounting to now resort –
The past fifteen years for you to define –
Where we find ourselves on the bottom line.

I know there is more for you to see –
Than the financial data known to me,
Like taxes, interest, all the rest –
That your accountant would know best.

But the final figure is in the black –
Since positive "in" overrides the slack,
Thus the monetary status is still ok –
For all projected bills to pay.

But there is a need to caution you –
The Merlin is seventeen years from new,
With increased age comes added cost –
Where gain to bottom line is lost.

Hot section or an engine overhaul –
On surplus balance could make call,
For engines don't forever last –
And failures just can't be forecast.

But of course they can be minimized –
When good practices are realized,
And as your pilot I've done that –
As will your new one – Captain Pat.

But this report should give relief –
The aircraft's fine, not causing grief,
It's really in great shape today –
And with Patrick it will stay that way.

So on that note report will end –
As with respect to you extend,
My thanks for what you've been to me –
In essence – my second – family.

09-23-1995

Complete

With last report now said and done –
As a new phase of my life begun,
These next few words will I extend –
In candor now as friend to friend.

For fifteen years I've been on call –
As a Merlin Captain for you all,
In a Corporate and a family plan –
Was how our flying first began.

And then from need we made a change –
The use of the aircraft rearrange,
I suggested to help the time line flow –
That to charter status we should go.

When with my suggestion you agree -
A greater burden was placed on me,
And there were times I rued the day –
When tied to the whims of the FAA.

Within the regs that they dispense –
Was lost the rule of common sense,
At times was hard to understand –
The specious things that they demand.

The MEL, Ops Specs and such –
Along with Drug-Plan much too much,
Overburdened bureaucracy is un-denied –
It should be abolished or simplified.

But I've diverged from where began –
Diverged from thrust of original plan,
I sought to give with rambling thought –
What fifteen years with you has brought.

It brought your friends I liked so much –
The Hills, Mrs. Murchison, Raushers and such,
The Flawns, the Winters, Thornhills and more,
That shared their goodness, fine rapport.

It brought your family, Morin and Roy –
SuSu, Beth, Eddie – all whom I enjoy,
Yes all your family who with me invest –
Warmth of relations, always the best.

Give them my love and thank them all –
For many fond memories I will recall,
They are the cream – gracious, elite –
Made my life good, satisfying – complete

09-23-1995
McAlester, OK

The following was generated from another lesson given by a Master Teacher, Gus Stewart -- Gus: As always — you gave me something to think about. You were truly a source of energy.

Energy

There is a power infinite – that's been since time began,
A power great, creative – that made all things by plan.
This power is all surrounding – a mystic energy,
Consuming power pervading – the mind and soul in me.

I know there is this power – I feel it everywhere,
Its evidence is certain – in dynamics it does share.
The truth of life around me – sight, sound, smell and feel,
Expose but one small portion – that it chooses to reveal.

It reveals what is self-evident – those things of certainty,
What in life we all relate to – the known reality.
But that energy that is hidden – truth beyond what we can see,
Is the secret of the ages – yes a Godly mystery.

God to me is real and certain – God is energy displayed,
Is the source of all creation – and for purpose all this made.
I can feel God in my being – with this energy alive,
And my mind with force of logic – this brief poem of God derive.

09-24-1995

Next are thoughts on a Sunday School discussion led by a class member that was followed in the church service by the Senior Pastor's sermon on the same subject.

Luke 12:13-21

As I sat within the church today –
I heard what Preacher had to say,
The words in sermon he did preach –
Luke 12:13 thru 21 did teach.

Commitment was the theme he spoke –
With a parable the mind provoke,
From passages were read from Luke –
That material way of life rebuke.

In that sanctuary atmosphere –
He have a message strong and clear,
To Bible's teachings must submit –
And to will of God our life commit.

Yes it was easy there in peace –
Religious fervor to increase,
The touch of Holy Bible feel –
From message Preacher did reveal.

The sermon tried to help me out –
Enforce my faith, relieve my doubt,
The truth of Jesus to embrace –
His crucifixion put in place.

But a feeling deep inside of me –
Brought discomfort and uncertainty,
Discomfort from what I perceive –
And uncertainty with what believe.

It remained uncertain what believed –
So from my discomfort unrelieved,
Though I joined here in Christianity –
Pained me greatly my hypocrisy.

Yes hypocrisy for must confess –
True Christian faith I don't profess,
Yet seek the source from which I came –
So I join in this religious game.

I join with others truth to find –
In a fellowship to ease my mind,
And there to God who knows it all –
In Jesus name with Christians call.

As I knelt today within the church –
At communion rail my soul to search,
I felt within a force so strong –
Assuring me --- that here belong.

10-01-1995

The next two items were thoughts on the ongoing news
concerning the OJ Simpson debacle.

OJ

There was a great hero whose name was OJ –
Was accused of two murders right there in LA –
But before was arrested he led merry chase –
As was drove in white Bronco all over the place.

The evidence all pointed to him as the one –
So was placed in detention fore trial begun –
The DA was certain as trial began –
Would prove to the Jury that OJ the man.

Now OJ had money many lawyers he bought –
To diffuse all the proof that to trial was brought –
They found in one witness a plan to succeed –
With him planted in jury a racism seed.

Now the trial it lasted a very long time –
And the coverage on TV was really a crime –
Judge did his best to keep lawyers on track –
As truth of the evidence defense did attack.

Blood trail, the glove, in the bedroom a sock –
High paid attorneys with scorn they did mock –
With one racist witness they put into place –
In LA was on trial not murder but race.

When the trial was over OJ was set free –
The jury no truth in the evidence did see –
Reactions are mixed as he goes on his way –
Was justice delay with no juice for OJ?

10-03-1995

With more thoughts, I modified the above to the following ---

The Ballad of OJ

There was a sports hero, a smoothing OJ –
Was accused of two murders right there in LA –
The evidence all pointed to him as the one –
So was placed in detention before trial begun.

But before was arrested he led merry chase –
As was drove in white Bronco all over the place –
Then the DA was certain as trial began –
They would prove to the jury that OJ their man.

Well OJ was smart and slick lawyers he bought –
To diffuse all the proof that to trial was brought –
Johnny found in one witness a plan to succeed –
Then with Furman he planted a racism seed.

The trial was grueling it lasted long time –
And the coverage on TV was worst than a crime –
Judge Ito tried hard to keep lawyers on track –
As truth of the evidence our Johnny attack.

The blood trail, the gloves and in bedroom the sock –
Those high paid attorneys with scorn they did mock –
With the specter of Furman they put into place –
Now in LA on trial was not murder but race.

Well the trial finally over with OJ set free –
That jury no truth in the evidence did see –
So reactions are mixed as he goes on his way –
Was there justice delayed with no juice – to OJ?

10-03/05-1995

Thoughts sitting in the balcony during Sunday service follow:

Blind

As I sat within the church today –
My mind in focus would not stay,
My thoughts to many things did stray –
As I joined with others there to pray.

In the church up in the balcony –
What from that vantage I could see,
Impact my mind and then set free –
The jumbled thoughts inside of me.

The sounds in church that I did hear –
Were pleasing, soothing to my ear,
Hand Bell Choir with chimes so clear –
Their joyful voice my heart endear.

Prayer of Confession then was read –
And words of assurance by Pastor said,
Then full church choir in hymn was led –
All enforced what to my mind was fed.

A Parable was heard by the congregation –
From Mathew, the Bible, came dissertation,
Then the preacher from his pulpit station –
In this sermon with Parable made relation.

My mind these things did analyze –
Their depth and purpose to apprise,
I sought an understanding wise –
To strip from God his earth disguise.

Yes I tried to keep an open mind –
What from church balcony would find,
But thoughts to service did not bind –
My view of God still dim, still --- blind.

10-08-1995

The Rotary Club I was a member of would accept donations at
the beginnings of meetings with statements of why the donation
was being given. I donated with the following ---

Oughter

Tonight four dollars I will give –
Because I think I oughter,
To celebrate a girl I love –
Samantha, my grand-daughter.

I use this forum at Rotary –
As a way for me to gloat,
On the birthday of a four year old –
A child on whom I dote.

10-12-1995

Next were thoughts on a motivational talk given by Rotary
District Governor at that time, Dr. Gonzalo Garza.

Slurp & Burp

Our dinner speaker did provoke –
Rotarian's do more than talk,
Members just can't slurp and burp –
they have to walk the walk.

Now the Slurp and Burp Rotarian –
by the speaker was defined,
As someone who has joined the club –
just to be wined and dined.

But the Slurp and Burp Rotarian –
we can't afford to do without,
They re integral to the structure –
to give the club its clout.

If they follow rules established –
with their dues and all the rest,
And support Rotarian projects –
in the ways that they know best.

Then as Rotarians they are needed –
if meetings they can make,
For we're all not meant as leaders –
may not want helm to take.

Each one to the club is important –
so long as the standards meet,
In fellowship should be welcomed –
if slurp and burp – is discreet.

10-12-1995

Have a sister-in-law who had terrible motion sickness. The
following relates to that.

Puke

With Jim and Katie and Mollie too –
We drove to Lake Travis in hopes to view –
The sun would be setting out in the West –
Some time with each other out there invest.

We to the Oasis with some trauma arrive –
After winding miles of curves did drive –
And Katie bless her sweet little heart –
From her stomach contents tried to part.

At first she thought would be all right –
That her motion sickness she could fight –
She was sure that it would be OK –
That she could make it all the way.

But in that assumption she was wrong –
Her motion sickness way too strong –
And only with great effort brave –
Did the contents of her stomach save.

Out at the lake she got off her feet –
Tried to convalesce as we without her eat –
On Oasis deck we watched sun set –
As Katie vainly tried her gut back get.

Jim, Mollie and Myrtle, along with me –
In our conversation we did all agree –
That it probably was a colossal mistake –
Our journey out to Lake Travis to make.

With sun in the West into horizon sunk –
With food all gone and margaritas drunk –
We settled sick Katie back into the car –
Drove for Saltine crackers to a place not far.

The crackers it seemed an essential need –
Before on drive back to our home proceed –
The Saltine crackers Katie might console –
If her tummy the crackers could control.

Jim's drive back to Austin was not as long –
Seems my way to the Oasis was really wrong –
So the Bee Caves way I now strongly rebuke –
But I'm oh so thankful Katie didn't --- puke.

10-17-1995

This next having to do with my youngest Grandson.

Pinkeye

One morning my Grandson whose name is Casey –
Woke up with the pinkeye, his momma called me –
At six in the morning she called quite distraught –
To tell me her darling the pinkeye had caught.

Now since was retired much free time I had –
The sense of that freedom it sure made me glad –
Was happy to know that this day I could share –
With sweet precious Casey ensconced in my care.

As a classical grandpa like a fool I behaved –
Got up from my bed and face I then shaved –
Did my ritual pushups, got dressed and then ran –
I drive to Circle "C" where continued the plan.

With A.J. and Casey we then went on our way –
Continued events that would shape this fine day –
Took A.J. to school and with Casey did drive –
Through the traffic of Austin to our house to arrive.

Now that sweet, perfect Casey so well did behave –
That my visiting in-laws on him did rave –
So that day is now over and when they said good-bye –
I hope they don't leave with a dose of pinkeye.

10-17-1995

For three nights in a row I had repetitive dreams. They were
not erotic dreams; rather religious – questioning – explorative
dreams. In the dreams I couldn't quite make out who or just
what was talking to me and pulling me towards something good.
The Beautiful Dreamer music, but not the words, were
predominant in the dreams. Thus the following –

Dreamer

Beautiful dreamer you came to me –
There in my sleep did your vision I see,
Drawn to the warmth or your lovely face –
Reached for the touch of your eager embrace.

Ah my sweet dreamer as dream begun –
You offered rapture before dream was done,
Lift my desires to heights up above –
Fanned my deep passion with offer of love.

Beautiful dreamer when I awake –
Stay in my memory my thoughts don't forsake,
Wrapped in your love with you long to stay –
Here in the night and in dream of the day.

Ah my sweet dreamer light of my soul –
You are the promise that makes my life whole,
You are the hope my dreams to set free –
Beautiful dreamer you beckon to me.

Beautiful dreamer stay in life's dream with me.

10-20-1995

Thoughts from briefly watching an event on TV.

Offense

I watched a lady preacher on TV –
With her preacher husband there to see,
And as I did thought golly gee –
I hate these ugly thoughts in me.

I felt my mind I had to clean –
From what I viewed upon the screen,
Thoughts I had were quite obscene –
In fact some really downright mean.

Her garish dress and hair coiffure –
Gave her an image far from pure,
Too hard for me to watch, endure –
All religious thoughts in me obscure.

Yes my good senses were abused –
But Myrtle and Mollie were amused,
So changing the channels in fun refused –
As from the room my person excused.

Now at the computer I try to dispense –
Words in rhyme that make some sense,
With thoughts irreligious so intense –
I hope my God takes no offense.

10-22-1995

This next is another written relating to the Rotary Club I was a
member of. We had a member that won the raffle held at each
meeting rather frequently. Thus the following.

Save

Last week a club member asked of me –
To come up with some meaningful poetry,
To immortalize who the raffle had won –
And in good nature to poke some fun.

It should be and easy poem to write –
The exploits of Wayne Hall to cite,
For the members here all realize –
He's got a monopoly on the raffle prize.

Our ole Ex-Pres does seldom lose –
No matter who the tickets choose,
And Wayne of course don't give a hoot –
He smiles and bows and takes the loot.

Now Wayne is a guy that I sure admire –
But of his winning spree I really tire,
So in the drawing tonight I wish him well –
But if he wins he can go straight to --- hell.

Hell is that place for people who sin –
And players like Wayne who raffles win,
I'm sure they cavort with evil Gods –
Explains why in raffles he beats the odds.

Well tonight to Wayne – that reprobate –
Five bucks to the Rotary will donate,
Not for the prize but to say I gave –
In order for Wayne from the Devil to save.

10-25-1995

During my Air Force career I was stationed at Laredo Air Force
Base for 4 years from 1964 to 1968. We have had reunions with
many friends from that time period over the years and the
following two were written during one of those reunions.

Laredo Reunion 95

A toast this day did I prepare –
To Air Force friends for whom I care,
To characters who shaped my past –
To cherished bonds I hope will last.

Last night upon a bus did go –
To Diamond W Ranch both to and fro,
There in Bandera to relate –
As we watched a show and Bar-B-Cue ate.

Of course Had took center stage alone –
He refused the aid of a microphone,
And there in his commanding voice –
He made pronouncements really choice.

The show went on with lots of fun –
Tricks with bull, and rope, and gun,
And a Western band that was "A" OK –
With corny jokes that all dismay.

But some of us also with ham engaged –
As our acting talents we assuaged,
Upon the stage did strut our stuff –
With performing talents really rough.

Now one who earned it made my day –
When role of a horse thief had to play,
He laughed at the part was given me –
That quick draw artist you did see.

Well back to the Hilton we did ride –
In our party room to get back inside,
And there in talk with memories sweet –
The fullness of the day complete.

Now tonight, to our hosts, to Steely Blue –
Joe, Jim, Dick, Had --- to all of you,
From the fastest gun? out in the West –
I raise a glass --- you are the best.

10-28-1995

Fifth

Our fourth reunion we survive –
We now must plan for number five,
And those two Hunts the Ron and Don –
That task have set themselves upon.

Last night that to me they relate –
They both, I think, thought Ninety-eight,
Would be the date this would occur –
Unless another year prefer.

A questionnaire Don did prepare –
With the Laredo Gang he hoped to share,
To try to set a time and place –
The majority thought we could embrace.

I pledged to them if they persist –
With all their planning I'd assist,
It would be good of them indeed –
If in this effort they would lead.

The Lanes, the Taylors, Kobericks too –
All volunteer their part to do,
So with this start I propose two toasts –
To our present and our future hosts.

10-29-1995
San Antonio
Hilton Hotel, Airports

This next was written in a silly mood. It was begun in an
ophthalmologist's waiting room with too much time on my
hands, and then completed on my arrival back home.

Eye

Eye went to an Ophthalmologist to see –
How well with my eyes Eye could see,
Eye went there to give my eyes a check –
And Eye found my patience Eye had to check.

Eye made the appointment well on time –
Eye thought eye check would take no time,
Eye entered a foyer with lots of room –
Then Eye was led to the eye exam room.

Receptionist and Eye some eye data then took –
With eyes on charts Eye little time took,
Yes Eye in good nature to receptionist made eyes –
As she professionally checked my eyes.

With her part done Eye stayed she left –
Eye eyed her go out the door turn left,
Eye thought that soon the Doc would see –
And Eye would know how well Eye'd see.

Eye stayed in room where eye exam done –
Eye had to stay for eye check not done,
Seems Eye had into the Doc's eyes to look –
To make this eye exam most officially look.

With eyes dilated Eye waited some more –
The Doc it seems eye patients had more,
Was about an hour before Eye Doc came in –
In my eyes Eye suppress bad mood I was in.

Eye exam complete Eye with prescription left –
Eye with wide eyes and what patience was left,
Eye groped down the hall the eye debit to pay –
As Eye promised no more will Eye for waiting pay.

11-01-1995

Back to Rotary. For one meeting we had two speakers who were
Organizational Change Consultants. They spoke on Change
and Development Facilitation. My thoughts on that follow.

Myths

Last night at Rotary we were told –
That business must use process bold,
Fixed modes of operations break –
And with the pieces new mold make.

From myths of old must be untied –
With forward vision new things tried,
Then as the pieces re-arranged –
May find that for the best were changed.

Our speakers with us this relate –
Through a handout they did validate,
Seven values there upon a sheet –
That would help a business to compete.

"Everybody counts" how the values began –
And that was theme how the lecture ran,
We learned through examples that they share –
Success will come if for people you care.

From one and the other we did hear –
A cohesive message loud and clear,
In this changing age in which we live –
Creative thought to the future must give.

I agreed with most of what they spoke –
But don't try to fix what isn't broke,
That's not to say you shouldn't refine –
But please – the problem first define.

And those old myths you can't discard –
Or you may learn lessons very hard,
For they were shaped from paradigm –
To ignore them could bring lesson grim.

So last night again we all did learn –
As from two good speakers we discern,
That communications holds the key –
And it's found right here – in Rotary.

11-03-1995

This next was my tongue in cheek response to a dear and close
friend that I had just received a letter from.

Dear -----, Excuse my silliness', but couldn't resist. I liked your letter, and assure you, with your help and others, we will try to be at an exceptional place for what we want to accomplish. I am enclosing a letter for your information that I am sending to our leader. As you can see, we have a good financial start towards the next. I do appreciate and need your support. Enjoyed seeing you and look forward to our next meeting - somewhere!
Sincerely, The Boss

El Supremo

From a fearless leader, glorious, brave –
To his lowest follower, worker, slave,
I've read your scribbling, infantile thought –
And in its simplicity my brilliant mind caught.

It's given that I'm so much smarter than thee –
So it shocks me to know that I do agree,
With the points in the babble I got from you –
Though I'm sure unintended you somehow got thru.

The points that you raised created no strain –
They obviously came from your gut not your brain,
Your gut is much larger than brain's tiny space –
But your leader has put points into proper place.

Now my status in life I am glad that you praise –
So slave I'll consider the points that you raise,
Your plusses and minuses I will keep well in mind –
And as your El Supremo the right place will find.

11-09-1995

I was requested by a Sunday School Faith Class member, Sharon Davis, if I would put into rhyme my thoughts on our Faith Class and its history. I did that on a vacation with the following ----

Faith Class

Within this close and kindred class –
We've watched the many years to pass,
As "Young Adults" we first began –
To "Faith Class" then with time we ran.

The "Middle Class" came in between –
To conform with changing status seen,
And throughout the years upon the role –
Each honored name made Faith Class whole.

With name we see a cherished face –
A persona good with warmth and grace,
And we treasure each, each listed name –
With all the strength that from it came.

That's why to "Faith Class" we return –
Here in fellowship we join and learn,
Those things in life that balance give –
To help us with our life to live.

Bob Duke was leader at the start –
Who taught with wisdom and the heart,
From books with meaning he select –
Our thoughts on God he tried perfect.

As leader then we each take turn –
To guide the class, discuss and learn,
But before the lesson can begin –
Off, On – the lights to quell the din.

Then noisy greetings members share –
Subsides as now we take our chair,
So the waiting teacher can proceed –
This vocal class to try to lead.

The thoughts within discussion sown –
They do not come from one alone,
They come from each somehow combine –
With thrust of lesson to align.

So "Faith Class" truly is a gift –
That gives to us a Spiritual lift,
And beloved departed, those still here –
Support our "Faith" – that God is near.

11-21-1995 (Wakulla Springs Lodge - in Florida)
11-23-1995 (Leesburg, Florida - my sister's home)
11-30-1995 (Gulfport, Mississippi - Comfort Inn)

What will follow will be a FAX I had sent to Liz Carpenter that
contained an email message received from a friend of mine that
was a take-off on Dr. Seuss style poetry. It had to do with the
politics of the day concerning Neut Gingerich and was titled
"The Gingrich that Stole Congress". The FAX to Ms. Carpenter
began

Liz:

Know you probably have this already, but wanted to make sure.
Hope you enjoy it if you haven't seen it. My response follows ----

Newt the Beaut

The apologies to Dr. Seuss –
Was not sincere was only ruse,
To nuke the Newt was poem's intent –
As shown within the lines were sent.

First line in diatribe was writ –
Was really just a bunch of s - - -,
To say EVERY Rep somewhat like Bill –
No credence in the poet instill.

Now pardon me for being uncouth –
But poet played loose with the truth,
The incessant use of hate, hate, hate –
The poet's deportment did negate.

Still must admit was kind of cute –
Though many lines were convolute,
For message rambled from the start –
Took Newt and Bill and the country apart.

But Ray I liked your "e" mail a lot –
The play on words from it I got,
With the viciousness of its attack –
It shows that Newt is right on track.

And Newt I think will get his due –
Though our government is now askew,
Who knows he just may meet the test –
When as President --- becomes the BEST!!!

(TONGUE-IN-CHEEK)

12-02-1995

This next is beyond being silly. It began with the following note:
Hi y'all -- Just experimenting with the net and seeing if I can get
through to multiple addressees. What I chose to try it with may
or may not be too fitting. But you know me I am not very
discriminating. Anyway, let me know if y'all got it. Not the gist
of the message, but the MESSAGE!
Wonder if Gus meant this as "pondering" ?

Simple Thoughts

It's the simple things in living –
that I for granted use,
Like the paper there beside me –
so my senses don't abuse.

This thing on which I'm sitting –
on which I perch each day,
Is device that's oh so essential –
to flush the debris away.

Even the water that's provided –
piped here from the lake,
Is a necessity to the process –
of this interval I take.

This room with space so private –
in home where it is fixed,
Supports this must do endeavor –
where service, nature mixed.

Electrons thru power lines flowing –
that into this house now run,
Earn most the praises now offering –
essential ere project begun.

This mobile phone here beside me –
not having a tie to a line,
Another convenience insuring –
no one can my need undermine.

These heavy thoughts I ponder –
ending my reign on the throne,
I'm secure that no one is watching –
at peace, contented – alone!!

12-05-1995

This next note came after the poem that follows: We learned
yesterday that a sweet friend, Frances Johnson, passed away
rather suddenly. We didn't know Frances extremely well, but
we knew her well enough to like and love her. The poem reflects
my inner feelings for her that I know are shared by all who
knew her. She was a vibrant and expressive lady.

Frances

Frances was a dear gentle lady,
who was loved by everyone –
A sweet and a gracious person,
the hearts of all she won.

With a smile was always happy,
took all from life she could get –
Reflecting the warmth in her nature,
she liked everyone she met.

Will miss this lady of sunshine,
her radiance of goodness, love –
Know she is making God happy,
as she smiles with God up above.

12-07-1995

I had a dear and elderly lady friend who had lost her husband
and was having a re-awakening of a relationship for another
marriage. She, and he, were troubled with their advanced age
on how far with the relationship to go. This next written to her.

Gather

Gather yea rosebuds while yea may –
by the pen of a poet was written,
For the eyes of a lady that he loved –
a lady with whom he was smitten.

The words of the poem that he wrote –
gave a message with no mistaking,
Told of the poets feelings of love –
that this lady in him was awaking.

Love like a flower has season to bloom –
a season in which it will flower,
A season controlled by the energy found –
those elements in life that have power.

When a man and a woman this energy share –
for each other they have this attraction,
If they are not kids by hormones possessed –
rose should blossom with loves interaction.

Their mind and their heart both should control –
let their strength of relationship carry,
The burden of whether this flower they now hold -
can be nurtured with time when they marry.

12-10-1995

Next was another visit with Grandsons to Discover Zone in
Austin, Texas.

Dumb

I think sometimes my brain goes numb –
When things I do are really dumb –
Like at DZ with my Grandson –
When he asked to show me what was fun.

He nimbly ran into the maze –
I followed him with mind in daze –
Through obstacle that twist and turned –
You'd think by now I would have learned.

He sprinted quickly in the lead –
My protestations didn't heed –
For him it was an easy pace –
For me it was a survival race.

At last we went down roller slide –
And left those tortures there inside –
With all my aches I took my seat –
A.J. refreshed – but I – was beat.

Then Myrtle she could not resist –
Went into maze with his assist –
She followed him upon her knees –
Her childish impulse to appease.

When all was done we did compare –
To see what from the maze we share –
With aches and pains we realize –
That's not a place for kids our size.

And so I proved I'm still a nut –
With aching knees and aching butt –
I proved once more with bottom numb –
Sometimes I do things --- really dumb.

12-16-1995

This next was written in Houston, Tx concerning a family drive
to view Christmas lights/decorations, and then a visit to Discover
Zone with the granddaughters.

Lights

With my granddaughters here at D.Z. –
I probe the thoughts I find in me,
From Toys-R-Us we made our way –
To this loud place where now they play.

Last night's events when fun began –
With Christmas lights a part of plan,
This Halie's big debut –
Her first ballet that we review.

Tamales grownups ate at home –
Before the city streets we roam,
But Heather and Halie wanted not –
Gary's tasty tamales that we got.

So to McDonalds we all went –
Where on Chicken Nuggets money spent,
From there we drove to see the sights –
The dazzle of the Christmas lights.

Oh what a joy it was last night –
The lights of Christmas gave delight,
The neighborhoods that we did drive –
Made our Christmas Spirit come alive.

There were a million lights at least –
On which the eye and mind could feast,
And the children with their Christmas song –
Gave night a festive feeling strong.

At times of drive we did extend –
It seemed the lights would never end.
Each city block was so complete –
As for Christmas honors they compete.

At last with all our hearts aglow –
To the Bullin house again did go,
For Granma Bullin needed a break –
The call for resting had to take.

It was kinda late when time for sleep –
And I made a promise now I keep,
That is why we're here today –
My promise of the night to pay.

It's nearing time to leave this place –
And I see the glee on happy face,
The pizza, popcorn, happy smile –
Has made this venture all worthwhile.

We'll press on with this hectic plan –
And make our way to Gary's van,
Then there with my granddaughters three –
Try hard to regain ---- my ---- sanity!!!

12-16-1995
Houston, Tx (Discovery Zone)

This next, as many others, was written in our church balcony.

Waiting

Tis the season of Christmas – as in church I now sit,
Observing the Cross – and the candles here lit.
The Choir Bell offering – for us does now ring,
To imbue us with spirit – that season does bring.

The congregation applauds – when the bell sound is done,
To express the emotions – Bell Choir has won.
A prayer gave in offering – then followed by song,
As the choir, congregation – sing Noel with voice strong.

Then the preacher with wife – alternate and recite,
A story of Christmas – that brings us delight.
A story of waiting – with all it details,
The many facets relating – to what waiting entails.

The waiting for good things – or things that are bad,
The waiting for joys – or alas, those things sad.
The voice of the preacher – the voice of his wife,
The vignettes they related – showed the waiting in life.

The waiting essential – for life to succeed,
As we move in the process – God's calling to heed.
The recitation was over – with the ending exposed,
And the source of all waiting – to us was disclosed.

For waiting in truth – by our Maker's design,
Giving meaning and purpose – towards and ending --- Divine.

12-17-1995

This next note to Rotary followed by poem "I Raise"

Brad: I doubt if I can make the meeting Thursday. I will
probably be in Rochester, N.Y. attending services for my sister.
I made a make-up today at the Down Town Club. Anyway, give
my greetings to all and look forward to seeing y'all NEXT
YEAR!!! HAPPY HOLIDAYS!!!

I Raise

To all club members, guests and such – I offer Christmas cheer,
I wish for you so very much – in this upcoming year.
Within these thoughts I give to you – I offer from the start,
My gratitude for what you do – and say it from my heart.

I want to make you all aware – of what you mean to me,
That I am proud of what we share – the goals of Rotary.
Four-way test that shapes the mold – on each of us bestowing,
Strong convictions that we hold – and where the club is going.

With Ninety-four now near its close – a new year on us falling,
Thoughts in rhyme on you impose – on your good graces calling.
Your excellence makes impact strong – deserving of great praise,
So to this club where I belong – a toast, a toast ---- I raise.

12-19-1995

After a lengthy illness, my oldest sister Carmella passed away at
her care facility in Florida. My brother-in-law Sam had her
body transported to Rochester, NY where she would be buried.
The next three poems were my thoughts of the moment.

Release

Dearly beloved ---- come join with me to pray,
For a wife, a sister, mother – we honor here today.
For Carm who gave to others – the comfort of her love,
And now shares that love with Jesus – in heaven up above.

In this holy time of Christmas – we pray with but one voice,
To the memory of this lady – whose life we now rejoice.
A life of great example – that met the highest test,
With the teachings of the bible – her energies invest.

As we worship in this season – when baby Jesus born,
We celebrate her living – as her passing also mourn.
Mourn that she has left us – rejoice she is in peace,
With angels that surround her – from her body found release.

Where her body knows no torment – the Spirit there no more,
For was called by our Creator – to a place its known before.
To the place of all beginning – where the Spirit truly free,
In the protecting arms of Jesus – safe for all Eternity.

12-20-1995 (Austin)
12-21-1995 (Continental Flight from Houston to Newark)

Celebrate

I'm here in Newark on my way,
To Rochester respects to pay.
The weather's caused a flight delay,
Who know I maybe here to stay.

My prospects here seem really grim,
The waiting room is full to brim.
Good nature strained up to the rim,
And demeanor anything but prim.

Departure announcements that I hear,
Is not sweet music to my ear.
Each new pronouncement makes it clear,
Substantiates my greatest fear.

The Ticket Agents do their best,
Anxieties to put to rest.
I try hard not to be a pest,
Although my patience put to test.

A father sitting next to me,
His little child plain to see.
Has need a private place to be,
From nasty diaper to be free.

He asked if I would save his seat,
So his little child he could make neat.
I thought that offer hard to beat,
To make the atmosphere more sweet.

Announcements still their gloom foretell,
that outbound flights not going well.
I think that some their soul would sell,
For an immediate seat on a plane to hell.

The thought of hell now brings me back,
To this terminal with people pack.
From wall to wall together stack,
In a waiting room that gives no slack.

And this confusion that I find,
Brings good diversion to my mind.
From thoughts of sadness I unwind,
To events surrounding now I bind.

At last to the aircraft as thoughts proceed,
Along the lines inside they heed.
As new events my mind now feed,
To analyze, examine, read.

Out to the plane we rode in bus,
That had no room for all of us.
A fellow traveler lightly cuss,
Most were delighted and didn't fuss.

I've been in this same fix before,
A circumstance we all deplore.
It cuts into our very core,
Emotions that we all abhor.

We're off the ground and up in flight,
I feel a sense of pure delight.
Although we're late in dark of night,
Now all it seems is going right.

Today was just a day to bear,
To make a journey here to there.
There was no day that I could spare,
To show my love for one I care.

I'll try to put my mind to rest,
My strength of will put to the test.
A faith in God to now ingest,
And Spirit of Christmas to fully digest.

By Spirit of Christmas to be taught,
Give thanks to God for what is wrought.
And to this venture in which am caught,
Honor my sister with loving thought.

In Rochester though hour is late,
With closest of family I relate.
With a sumptuous dinner that we ate,
My sister's life we ----- celebrate.

12-21-1995 (Continental Express Flt. from Newark to Rochester)
12-22-1995 (Early morning in Rochester)

A Need

I'm leaving now back home to go,
From Rochester, the cold, the snow.
I watch outside the winter show,
And anxieties begin to grow.

The weather still controls my fate,
With Christmas season does relate.
The flights again are running late,
Delaying time we leave the gate.

All my connections seem alright,
The Newark change is not too tight.
If leg to Houston on-time flight,
Should land in Austin by midnight.

I find a need to write this verse,
Here with myself on page converse.
Since hands of time I can't reverse,
I still with mind can past traverse.

Go back in time and there to find,
My oldest sister in my mind.
To see what thoughts to memory bind,
What past events will now unwind.

And ah the love she gave to all,
Sweet, sweet the memories I recall.
Her passing on has cast a pall,
Could make the tears to quickly fall.

But tears my energies would drain,
Open wounds that bring more pain.
Yet not one thing can they explain,
Thus tears are useless – shed in vain.

Her death like silent, heartless thief,
Stole my control I felt my grief.
But I fought hard to make tears brief,
Took back my poise, regained relief.

The tears that in my eyes did start,
I forced back into aching heart.
And emotions that were torn apart,
Restored when tears from eyes depart.

My thoughts now take a different turn,
From announcement giving me concern.
For over the speaker I just learn,
This night to Austin may not return.

The Continental Rep in terminal state,
That the flight to Houston very late.
So Austin won't be made this date,
With new travel plans must now relate.

After Ticket Agents I did wart,
On my daughter's good graces I resort.
With her in Houston I'll make it short,
Put a temporary halt --- to this report.

12-22/23-1995

Again, that previous poem was begun in the Rochester Airport
Terminal then continued off and on between Rochester to

Newark to Houston and then completed in Spring, Texas at my daughter's home where I remained till after Christmas. My wife drove there from Austin by herself so we could spend that Christmas time together as family.

This next was written in response to a Christmas Greetings received by my son-in-law Gary from a friend of his who lived in the Rio Grand Valley there in South Texas. I wrote the response to it and we send it to his friend, from the Bullin family.

Cheer

Your greetings from the Rio Grande –
Is a poem we love and understand,
By your sense of rhyme were we impressed –
And the lovely thoughts within expressed.

Your message of Christmas is quite a feat –
With a flow of words that is complete,
Our appreciation to you we now extend –
Through Gary Bullin who is your friend.

We read your poem late last night –
And it gave to us such warm delight,
The spirit of Christmas there did find –
Through the insight of your poet's mind.

We are glad you're both on Texas land –
You add stature to the Rio Grande,
And we wish you two a lot of cheer –
Seasons greetings and a "HAPPY NEW YEAR"!!!!

12-24-1995 (Spring, Texas)

Still enjoying the Christmas Holiday with family follows.

Compete

On Christmas Eve in Ninety-five –
A glut of food I did survive,
With Mary and Gary where I did stay –
I ate and ate and ate all day.

At times the burps did me assault –
But then I knew it was my fault,
For my will-power I had put to bed –
As I ate a mass of food instead.

Gary's mom and I we both compete –
To see which one the most could eat,
I think I ate much more than her –
The way my guts inside me stir.

But I awoke this morning rather glad –
For last night no indigestion had,
With no misfortunes now to tell –
The wait for Santa went quite well.

Today more willpower I'll try to use –
So my eating habits I won't abuse,
From piggish instincts I will break –
Be selective with my food intake.

I'll try to watch my diet today –
As with their toys the children play,
And with family members won't compete –
For on even terms we together do eat.

12-25-1995
Mary and Gary's - Spring, Texas

Next poem began with the following: Dear Joyce --- and Gus,

Myrtle and I want to thank you for a wonderful evening. We wouldn't have missed it for anything and like all who were there, we love and appreciate you --- both !!!

Appreciate

Tonight we all must raise our voice –
To a beautiful teacher really choice –
Her gift of teaching we rejoice –
In joy on her retirement – a toast to Joyce.

The toast to friends of yours I led –
Were partial thoughts within my head –
There were so many left unsaid –
Besides those off the napkin read.

There at Ruth's Chris upon my mind –
So many pleasant thoughts did find,
Your gentle grace, your manner kind –
The love that you to Gus does bind.

Now Gus to all is a man quite wise –
Strengthened by your marriage ties –
This retirement party his surprise –
A gift of affection to really prize.

Well enough of that I'll now relate –
For all those there who drank and ate –
The food and fun was really great –
But it's Joyce and Gus --- we appreciate!!!!

12-27-1995

The toast above was offered during a retirement party for Joyce Stewart at Ruth's Chris Restaurant. The party was given by her husband Gus and 60 people were in attendance. It was a great party for a great lady.

I wrote this next after spending time, again, with grandchildren at Discovery Zone.

Alien

I think at times I'm not from here –
I'm from a different atmosphere,
I'm here from another Galaxy –
This earth is not first home for me.

I don't know where to put the blame –
Why to this planet Earth I came,
Know not if I'm a Robot or man –
If flesh and blood or just tin can.

My Grandson says he's an alien too –
The two of us make quite a crew,
Of course I know he's partially right –
With my alien genes he's really bright.

My wife just laughs and humors me –
This terrestrial woman that I see,
There is no way for her to know –
My earthly side is all I show.

But I know somehow that I did ride –
From out in space to here collide,
And I know I tease an awful lot –
But that is how to earth I got.

Now when I look out there in space –
I try to find that other place,
In the million lights out there I see –
One special light is home to me.

I think some day that I will learn –
And to that place I will return,
Then I will be at home once more –
As whatever form I was before.

My grandson put these thoughts in me –
In discussion going to D.Z.,
And I hope with this he has some fun –
For alien thoughts in me are done.

12-29-1995

Oh Damn

I looked at this photo and said "Oh Damn" –
They're like three brothers Fred, Jim, Sam –
With two on one side and one on the other –
As close to me as was my older brother.

I like this crowd that I'm married to –
Including Mollie, Mary, Katie and Marilou –
And Bill Ley for sure a part of what to me –
Is best of good fortune - my wife's family.

My children, nieces, nephews then follow suit –
With their own children who are oh so cute –
Yes on and on I hope this cycle will go –
So the love in family unit can grow, grow, grow.

Here I am again with my thoughts to write –
In a poetry style may be trite, trite, trite –
But I hope my feeling are well understood –
"Oh Damn" an expression - at times that is good.

P.S. -- This was modified to please my wife who was defensive

12-30-1995

This next is the last poem I wrote in the year 1995 --- my
thoughts during a hastily planned New Year's Eve party.

Our Host

In the year of our Lord Nineteen Ninety-five –
As this past year we did survive,
Before the New Year does arrive –
It is our good fortune we're alive.

Thank God for friends so firm and tight –
For relationships that make life bright,
For all Creation good and right –
We praise His Name this New Year's night.

So thank you God for what we know –
For the blessings on us you bestow,
At the stroke of midnight to you our Host –
Please don't be offended – we raise – A TOAST !!!!

12-30-1995

My wife and I began the New Year by responding to an urgent request from our local Blood Bank for her "O" Negative blood type. I went with her and also gave. I was impressed by the professionalism and efficiency of the staff and wanted to thank them for tolerating, with such good humor, my silliness while there. I wrote the next thoughts that follow and mailed it to them. I later received a very pleasant and positive response from their Executive Director.

Blood

Today with my wife some blood I gave –
At a place where blood they take and save,
The lowered the level in my tank –
And drained it into their blood bank.

Before they did they subjected me –
To an interrogation - more a third degree,
On sex and drugs and life style overdone –
But at my age --- it was kind of fun.

Then to a padded couch I was politely led –
Where my finger was pricked until it bled,
Pulse, Temperature and pressure were taken too –
Before they did to me what they had to do.

What they had to do can be considered mean –
Stuck me with a needle that I hoped was clean,
And after that shaft into my arm they feed –
The injector contentedly watched me bleed.

When all was done I weakly left the chair –
Almost lost my way getting out of there,
But they insist that I stay and rest a while –
And with great audacity they even smile.

Thanked me for coming and the blood I gave –
Said I need return and more of it save,
Course I nodded my head, dare not disagree –
I was in their clutches – too weak to flee.

01-04-1996

This next in fun to my daughter and son-in-law in Seattle.

Dear Myrtle and Bob

We're Coming

We're coming to Seattle –
Your cage we're gonna rattle,
Cause with you we will stay –
As around Seattle we play.

With Continental we'll be flying –
On your Boeing jets relying,
Gonna leave here just before 8 –
12:24 in Seattle is a minute late.

We know that you will be there –
Our on-time arrival to share,
We'll then drive out to your place –
To start our hectic pace.

We will call the Goff's in Tacoma –
And there one day we may roam-a,
We may plan with them one night,
If you think it would be alright.

But our schedule is totally free –
It's you two that we want to see,
So whatever your plans – we agree –
We are easy – your mother --- and me!!

See what happens when you don't respond quickly!!!

Love Daddy

01-07-1996

What follows was written during a Continental flight from
Houston to Seattle and then finished at the home of my daughter
& son-in-law in Seattle. I find a need at times to clear my mind
of extraneous and miscellaneous thoughts.

Growth

There's no one can explain to me –
The wonders in this world I see,
The deep emotions that I feel –
From what God chooses to reveal.

With the vistas coming to my sight –
My mind does wander here in flight,
It fails to focus in one place –
One line of thought it will not trace.

There's much on which the mind can play –
Too much on just one thought to stay,
This blessed land over which we fly –
With changing scenes that catch the eye.

The Texas plains, the mountains tall –
In their own voice my senses call,
Each their impressions on me make –
As my emotions they awake.

America this land I love –
When seen from here, from up above,
With open spaces oh so wide –
Gives sense of freedom un-denied.

This vast expanse of open land –
Makes it hard for me to understand,
The focused groups that overstate –
The perilous growth of our birth rate.

As from Texas to Seattle go –
The passing terrain to me does show,
There is abundant empty space –
To grow and prosper in this place.

My mind did not dwell here too long –
On the lighter side of life belong,
I looked there sitting by my side –
At the beauty of my sleeping bride.

I wasn't sure but it did seem –
She was in mid of a restful dream,
Her breathing soft with even pace –
With peaceful look upon her face.

I touched her hand and she did smile –
She squeezed me gently for a while,
And then my mind returned once more –
Outside the plane where was before.

My poet's obsession I did not fight –
I began on paper a poem to write,
To pass some time with thoughts in me –
And – record them in --- my – diary.

01-10-1996 (Continental flight from Houston to Seattle)
01-11-1996 (Myrtle & Bobs apartment there in Seattle)

This next, followed a discussion with my daughter Myrtle on
what the Spirit is or means.

The Spirit

The Spirit is an Energy –
A hidden force you cannot see,
A force that has no mass, no weight –
No physical properties to relate.

The Spirit is a mystical thing –
It has no teeth, no bite, no sting,
It can only make its presence known –
Through the human emotions of body shown.

For Spirit through this earth does pass –
As a Force within the body's mass,
Together bound with Creation's glue –
A bond of life between the two.

From Creation's power the Spirit came –
Where Creation and God are one and the same,
For the Power of God all things create –
And that same Power does liberate.

Yes energy creates all matter we see –
While matter destroyed creates energy,
Thus other dimensions I'm sure there must be –
And the Spirit is one – is God's Energy.

01-12-1996 (Seattle at Myrtle & Bob's home)

This next was a note that preceded what I had written and sent
in a letter to friends of ours in Tacoma that we stayed a night
with during our visit in Seattle.

Dear Peg and Sy,

We received your nice card today and want you to know how
much we enjoy our visits with you. I sent your girls' address
and such to my niece in the Big Apple and hope she and her
husband will be smart enough to call them. I think they would
all benefit. Anyway --- Sy – below is the poem I had started that
morning you came into the kitchen and gave me something else
to think about. We love you both and feel fortunate that fate, or
whatever, has allowed us the relationship.

Lakota Mother

Within this house where now I sit –
Is joy, and love, and lots of wit,
These are the first things come to mind –
With many other thoughts I find.

In house of Goff with lovely view –
With nothing better now to do,
I'm in a reflective mood to write –
A poem somber, thoughtful, light.

I'm in Tacoma it's Sunday morn –
I watch a new grey day be born,
And as it's born with what I see –
The good in life takes over me.

With Peg and Sy dear friends I know –
The gracious love to all they show,
The special inner gifts they share –
Are here around me everywhere.

A form of bronze does regal stand –
To grace this home, majestic, grand,
An eagle with its wings outspread –
That soars above a maiden's head.

The Indian maiden I see there –
To indomitable spirit of Peg compare,
The perils found in life both brave –
And with strong Spirit life to save.

With ailment that not hers to choose –
In treatment Peg her hair did lose,
Though Sy her baldness he does tease –
With support of love his Peg does please.

Of all the things that here abound –
The music, writings, pictures found,
The greatest gift of all I see –
Is the strength within this family.

The eagle soaring there in flight –
With Lakota mother holding tight,
Within this home it does belong –
As a testament – to Spirit strong.

01-14/18-1996

Begun at Goff's home in Tacoma and then completed in Austin

What follows next is the recap of an enjoyable meeting at our
University Area Rotary

PHD (Lemon Meringue Pie)

Last Thursday night at our Rotary –
Many of us were entertained by a PHD,
Those around the table where I sit –
Were stimulated by a Physicist's wit.

Susie Malone she great fun did make –
With a tale about a pie she bake,
The favorite pie of a friend she knew –
What that pie in the past led him to do.

Seems a vacuum cleaner in his youth –
Was the catalyst to things uncouth,
His mother's neighbor did entice –
An innocent lad to do things not nice.

Was a broken vacuum took him there –
A Lemon Meringue pie was the bill-of-fare,
He was offered the pie for him to taste –
If he pleasured the lady and became unchaste.

Now Dirk when the story he had heard –
Looked on his youth as quite absurd,
He thought his teen age years were great –
Until Lemon Meringue story Maloney relate.

Some others around the table spoke –
One asked how often the vacuum broke,
Susie told of attachments the vacuum had –
That required return of this hapless lad.

The raffle that evening, a vinegar thing –
In suggestive bottle more jokes did bring,
At our table the winner although amused –
The bottle, risqué, he politely refused.

All eyes were on Susie our fun PHD –
She drew a new number for all to see,
The humor continued with devilish design –
Drew her own ticket that end in six-nine.

Remainder of evening by speaker was done –
An excellent speaker who accolades won,
Spoke of how drugs does behavior impact –
How society may pay if it doesn't react.

Speaker and Susie the evening made good –
Both in relation were well understood,
Susie gave humor, the speaker did teach –
Each to our intellect they tried to reach.

I'll end with assessment of drugs, Lemon Pie –
That they both are addictive I cannot deny,
Drugs stand alone, Lemon Meringue now to me –
Is addiction of choice, ask our own --- PHD.

01-20-1996

There were times the Rotary Club I was a member of would ask
a member to donate a prize to be raffled at a meeting. This next
poem relates to such an occasion when a gifted next door
neighbor of mine graciously helped me to do that.

Rattle

On my dear neighbor I again rely –
A raffle prize for the club to buy,
That gifted lady who lives next door –
Who helped me with this task before.

To her studio this morning as we went –
Where very little time was spent,
For there upon a shelf we found –
The perfect prize that will astound.

Rebecca Roberts with me share –
An interactive sculpture there,
A perfect rattle fired of clay –
For discriminating adults to admire and play.

Explanation of rattle sound is neat –
Because of the intensive heat,
Most material would with clay be fused –
So little clay beads inside are used.

Enough of what is offered here –
I just want to make it very clear,
This sculptured piece by artist made –
Is worth more than the price I paid.

01-25-1996

Troy

There was a precious little boy –
Grandnephew by the name of Troy,
He came here with his Grandpa Fred –
And by the nose his Grandpa led.

But Troy was lucky that he had –
A Grandpa always made him glad,
A Grandpa who would dote on him –
And cater to his every whim.

Troy's Grandma's name was Marilou –
Troy knew with her just what to do,
He knew the darling things to say –
To assure he mostly got his way.

Now little Troy was awfully bright –
Was on the go from morn till night,
His strength of will was very stout –
Of course it wore poor Grandpa out.

But Grandma use a different tact –
To insure her Grandson would react,
With gentle firmness she did reach –
Precocious Troy she tried to teach.

Her Grandson she would seldom tease –
But seems his whims she also please,
For as I watched Troy through the day –
He almost always had his way.

I enjoyed my in-laws being here –
With Troy I tried not interfere,
Like Fred I liked to tease a lot –
And with Marilou I thought best not.

Yes – Marilou and Fred were quite a pair –
With life of Grandson that they share,
And I have no doubt Troy understood –
His Grandma and Grandpa were good --- REAL GOOD!!!

02-02-1996

The following thoughts were jotted down during Sunday Service
in the Church balcony. Minor change made to the original.

Forever

There is no doubt that I will be –
Forever with Eternity,
That I forever will converse –
With the Forces of the Universe.

Forever here within this space –
The never ending future face,
With Spirit bond I cannot sever –
An Eternal link will last forever.

I know that this forever so –
That my Spirit will forever grow,
That my Spirit is an Energy –
From a Power that was and forever will be.

This endless Universe so vast –
Is timeless and forever will last,
As endless time does forever teach –
Understanding forever – is beyond my reach.

02-04-1996

This next is a re-write of my earlier on Rattle. There was a little
delay in the presentation of the sculpture. I took that time to
rewrite as follows:

Rattle Two

The raffle prize I brought tonight –
Is a sculptured piece of pure delight,
A piece of art to put on display –
By hand of an artist who works with clay.

On my next door neighbor I again rely –
This elegant prize for the club to buy,
That gifted lady who lives next door –
Who has helped me with this task before.

To her studio one morning we went –
Where very little time was spent,
For upon a shelf we quickly found –
This perfect prize that will astound.

Rebecca Roberts with me did share –
This interactive sculpture there,
This perfect rattle fired of clay –
For adults like us to admire and play.

Explanation of rattle sound is neat –
Because of the intensive heat,
Most material would with clay be fused –
So little clay beads inside she used.

The shiny surface on which you gaze –
Comes from a black metallic glaze,
Upon clay surface the glaze applied –
Then with final firing become allied.

Allied in heat process they bond as one –
A Functional Sculpture when process done,
So rattle presented, this art form you see –
Is yours if you're lucky – and win it from me.

Well enough of what is offered here –
I just want to make it very clear,
This sculptured piece by great artist made –
Is worth far more than any price that's paid.

02-05-1996

Following were thoughts when preparing to go to a Valentine
Crazy Bridge get-together with our Sunday School Faith Class
at the church. I was getting ready for a shower and had put on
the bed a pair of red socks with white hearts, and a pair of white
shorts with red hearts that had "My heart beats for you" on
them. I couldn't resist putting the words that came to mind into
my collection of poems.

Hearts

Tonight I have upon my feet –
Red socks with white hearts very neat,
And on white shorts that I now wear –
Are red hearts scattered everywhere.

The socks you are allowed to see –
But shorts that alone for my wife can be,
On the hearts on shorts is printed clear –
"My heart beats for you" – my dear.

Now the socks and shorts came from my wife –
Who is the treasure of my life,
And tonight to her I want to say –
The socks and shorts have made my day.

02-10-1996

At that Valentine Crazy Bridge get-together with our Sunday School Faith Class, we exchanged Valentine Cards. This next relates to a humorous card that was given.

Sox

I heard a treatise on good sox –
Was written by a Word Smith Fox,
The meaning of the written word –
Gave double meaning once was heard.

That clever writer did entwine –
A play on words in Valentine,
And with word choices made no gaffs –
Provided lots and lots of laughs.

Expressed for sox we all have need –
And with report then did proceed,
To share a message loud and clear –
That sox meant more than did appear.

Now with that author won't compete –
The meaning given quite complete,
Though sox the subject was addressed –
For the Valentine message – get undressed!!!

10-11-1996

This next was another written in church balcony during the
service. It was a mixture of what I was hearing during the
service and a Sunday School session viewing a video
presentation of Church Reformation.

Reformation

The Reformation was a need –
For Christianity to proceed,
The Bible had to be transposed –
For words of Christ to be exposed.

"The Church" God's Bible did control –
With power absolute and whole,
It exercised command most stern –
When Church reformers did intern.

Reformers their own message preach –
With simple English they did teach,
The Scripture lessons they instruct –
From Bible version they construct.

Words of Christ they clearly taught –
With all the fervor in which caught,
And in so doing authority defied –
The Church their teaching then decried.

For wealth and power was church concern –
The reformers a threat as heretics burned,
And though the Church their word assailed –
Reformers succeeded and truth prevailed.

Christianity victorious, hierarchy wrong –
Thus the Church continues very strong,
But in the flock heretics still see –
One of them certainly --- has to be me.

02-11-1996

What next is the Post Script written as an afterthought at home
as I was getting into my files what I had written in the balcony.

PS

Yes me for I retain the hope –
That someday I will be the Pope,
At the Vatican the smoke will rise –
And I'll be Pope --- surprise, surprise.

Antonio Giuseppe the Pope of all –
To know God's thoughts on me must call,
For on this earth I'm now His Voice –
He speaks through me – rejoice, rejoice.

You know I say this tongue in cheek –
One goes to God direct to speak,
No one, no church – can truly teach –
With certainty --- how God to reach.

One has to look deep down inside –
What truths, what canons to abide,
And when your life on earth is done –
To learn what life in death is won.

02-11-1996

I had a good friend who just experienced a root canal procedure. He was and remains, a friend I enjoy discussion with.

Dear Jerry,

Not Me

The Dentist's scourge, a "ROOT CANAL" –
With all the pain it does entail,
That dreaded thing in Dentistry –
I'm glad it was done to you not me.

I heard from Peg about your plight –
And thought I'd give to you tonight,
Some words of cheer and sympathy –
But I'm glad it was done to you not me.

Like your President I'll make it plain –
Of course you know I feel your pain,
I have compassion for your misery –
Still I'm glad it was done to you – not me!!!

02-21-1996

Once again from the Church Balcony, I scribbled some thoughts generated during a Sunday School Faith Class presentation on a series being conducted on Church Reformation.

Reformation Two

Church reformation history,
Is one of pain and misery,
From authoritarian church control,
Reformers altered what was Church role.

So Scriptures by more Christians heard,
Transcribed to English Bible's Word,
Although that was the peoples gain,
Reformers died in anguished pain.

It's hard to fathom why God willed,
His faithful followers be killed,
What ugly things in His Name done,
Since Christian Faith on earth begun.

It makes no sense to me at all,
Why anyone on God would call,
With the reading of Church history,
And God's rejection that I see.

Now others view it differently,
In the death on Cross find victory,
That Jesus rising from the grave,
Is gift from God their soul to save.

But the Bible story I deplore,
I get from it a different score,
It shows me God hard to explain,
Who condemned His only Son to pain.

With Jesus death to say man saved,
To me a concept cruel, depraved,
The Reformation process also a blight,
Obscene and shows I may be right.

These words express my inner thought,
To Christian Church where I am caught,
One last thing to Christ will say,
If I am wrong – Your forgiveness I pray.

For I seek God's truth in Christianity,
To some this may sound like hypocrisy,
If with God You are One and all this did create,
Help me now find the way so with You can relate.

02-25-1996

This next written to my daughter and son-in-law in Seattle.

Easy

It's easy now for me to see –
You're asking for a poem from me,
When I don't find you on the net –
Another poem from me you get.

I know how busy you two are –
You drive Seattle wide and far,
To jobs at Boeing and Hospital you fly –
Then ski and climb those mountains high.

I'm sure that you enjoy all that –
Your leaky apartment and deformed cat,
All the beauty of the far Northwest –
Keeps you on the go with little rest.

But take the time from out your day –
With hi-tech computer sit down and play,
On the Internet link for us to see –
Send an e-mail message to your mom and me.

A Master's Degree would be worthwhile –
Upon our face it would put a smile,
It would give to us some peace of mind –
If career you liked it helped you find.

This poem I started another night –
You've both been great the way you write,
I just had a few minutes of idle time –
So some thoughts I send with love --- and rhyme.

Daddy

02-26-1996

This next was written in preparation for Sunday's Faith Class.

Meaning of Prayer

We know the meaning of prayer,
Communion with our God to share,
In the form of an earnest request,
When emotions are put to the test.

We usually pray when there's need,
For an event in our life to succeed,
It is mostly in an act of contrition,
As to God we make holy petition.

When in goodness of life we do bask,
With nothing from God for to ask,
Prayer may then not be supplication,
Rather thank you with joy and elation.

Thus meaning of prayer is well known,
In the essay by Lewis this was shown,
Discussion of prayer, not its meaning,
But instead, what from it, are we gleaning.

In his essay, The Efficacy of Prayer,
C.S. Lewis his thoughts with us share,
Though his logic is brilliant we see,
That no answers, no answers – has he.

02-27-1996

The next continues the projection of the last. It was written in preparation for a Sunday School Faith Class lesson I would be giving. The subject was the writing found in the C.S. Lewis essay Should the Bible Be Revised.

I answered that to myself at the time with "Of course it should".

Dear God

I'm thankful for your blessings –
for all you've given to me,
For the wealth of my good fortune –
the wonders in life I see.

Of you I have no understanding –
no certainty how to relate,
Except with my mind in communion –
through prayer in a religious state.

Threads of my life You have woven –
core of my being You surround,
Is bond that gives me full meaning –
where purpose for living is found.

I know not if the Bible true written –
Jesus Christ and Creator the same,
But I'll honor the teaching of story –
for I know from Your wisdom it came.

The times I've not heeded your calling –
the many things I've failed to do,
I'm aware of and makes me more cherish –
these blessings I know came from You.

So accept this the prayer I now offer –
my reverence of you oh so strong,
God m mind is at peace in this moment –
forgive me if thought in it wrong.

03-16-1996

At the Rotary I belonged to, members provided speakers for the
meetings. It was my pleasure and privilege to have two great
candidates to do that. This next describes who they are.

Miracle

Diana Sanchez – Bushong –
Spoke to us on religious song,
As she works towards her PHD –
In Musical Arts enrolled at UT.

Her husband to us last week spoke –
With his music our mind did provoke,
Not religious, least not till the end –
But to the commercial his music extend.

Diana and Tim are a pair –
The gifts of their talents they share,
Whether hymn or a jingle for selling –
Presentation each gave was compelling.

To our club a strong message did bring –
When we meet takes persuasion to sing,
Though we all raise our voice to the pledge –
For some reason towards singing we hedge.

I know what the problem is for me –
I sing with a voice that's off key,
I'm not one who with song would join in –
But I think with this Club could begin.

So a challenge I give now to you –
With the message received from these two,
From Tim and Diana Bushong –
There is much could be gained with a song.

After pledge I think someone should start –
Simple song we all know from the heart,
We may find it is fun and not pain –
That we've nothing to lose and may gain.

On someone who sings we should call –
By that, there's none other, Wayne Hall,
He should lead us in a song he incite –
At his urging one day I did write.

I attach it with no hope to succeed –
But if by strange chance we proceed,
To my shock we break out into song –
What a miracle God worked – through Bushong.

03-22-1996

Next was written for my last lesson to the Sunday Faith Class.

Spared

During month of March before this class –
As your teacher I have shown my br-ass,
With the C.S. Lewis lessons taught –
Your knowledge did increase by naught.

The month began with thoughts on prayer –
That Lewis through his essay share,
And with that lesson we agree –
That prayer remained a mystery.

Now second week with lesson done –
Your wealth of knowledge where begun,
Though C.S. Lewis writings great –
Thoughts therein I could not relate.

The third week went as those before –
With Lewis's writings I became a bore,
I'm sure I bit more than could chew –
In selecting Lewis to teach to you.

"The Grand Miracle" was my last stab –
As Lewis's coat tails tried to grab,
And that miracle as we all know –
Was the "Resurrection", what a show.

So today at last you can take a break –
For lessons from Lewis I now forsake,
As I thank you for the time we shared –
I know you're thankful from me to be ----
SPARED!!!!

03-30-1996

The Rotary Club I was the Treasurer for, to raise money, would
sponsor shows. Following a performance I wrote this next.

Members

You members of this Club I thank –
For getting money to the bank,
For all the efforts you invest –
To give this Club your very best.

The "Quilters" play was really fun –
And now that it is said and done,
Our treasury should have much more –
As we tally up the final score.

With all the members who were there –
That came with friends the night to share,
It's obvious that we succeed –
In assisting our financial need.

So thank you again for all you do –
It's nice to be in step with you,
It's really great for us to be –
Members of this close knit Rotary.

04-17-1996

At times I had need to explain to myself my need for poetry.
This next was just one of those time.

Inner Need

I find when putting rhyme in place –
A free thought process mind must trace,
Must play a word selection game –
To keep the words with thoughts the same.

As I write a poem I want no guess –
On thoughts I'm trying to express,
And some I know I might offend –
As words to thoughts I try to blend.

The sentence structure that I use –
At times word placement I abuse,
And this I'm sure is one such time –
As I put my thought with words to rhyme.

I know could be more properly said –
These rambling thoughts within my head,
This poetry – these thoughts I write –
I'm sure to many is trite, trite, trite.

But that's all right – OK – with me –
I have no delusions of great poetry,
My poetry's not for others to read –
It satisfies for me a deep --- inner need.

04-28-1996

Next is another from the Church balcony.

"Elijah"

Oh hear the sound the choir makes –
the beauty of the voices,
That gives sweet praise to God on high –
as God with choir rejoices.

Oh hear this work of Mendelssohn –
"Elijah" his creation,
The vibrancy found in every voice –
honors God with adoration.

The violins, the roll of drum –
the flute, the cello playing,
The clarinet, bassoon, string bass –
with viola God's Soul portraying.

Oh hear and feel the aura of God –
in the power now surrounding,
The healing power of sound and love –
within the church abounding.

I feel the urge these words to write –
with a force that's so exacting,
And I know, I know deep within my heart –
God is here and interacting.

04-28-1996

Next is something I wrote that I was not going to include. But,
since it still explains well a part of my affection, attraction and
deep love for my wife now of over 50 years, I included it.
It was for Mother's Day, the suit and the poem.

Suit of Black

When I saw you in that bathing suit –
The hormones in me all compute,
You looked so good in suit of black –
Most tempting as a tasty snack.

On you it looked so nice, nice, nice –
I'd pay for it most any price –
I hope you think the next not crude –
You only look better in the nude.

I gave that gift for Mother's Day –
Because it took my breath away,
From any side, the front, top, back –
You're perfect in that suit of black.

When that suit of black I see you wear –
I'll think I wasn't being fair,
That provocative thing is more for me –
I love it when you look ---- SEXY!!!

05-04-1996

The following is self-explanatory and written in Florida.

Cigars

They're long and brown and look like hell –
And when they're lit they really smell,
They're stogies and boy do they provoke –
As their substance all goes up in smoke.

Now of me my son-in-law made a request –
If when in Ft. Lauderdale I would invest –
Some time to see if were there displayed –
Cigars that in Castro's Cuba were made.

For these special cigars he did implore –
If were made in Havana he wanted four,
It seems to me a distasteful cause –
But of course I agreed with little pause.

In Ft. Lauderdale a small shop was found –
With cigars displayed there all around,
Since cigars from Cuba against the law –
No cigars from Havana in there I saw.

In this shop I thought my task was done –
But my wife's endeavors had just begun,
She knew our son-in-law's unique request –
And Castro's Cuba would not her best.

From out her purse there within her hand –
Came a list of cigars not of Cuban brand,
It was a formidable list of cigars to see –
And I knew four cigars soon were ours to be.

The smug shop owner proud of his high cost –
And my sense of humor on all was lost,
When with the odds I could not compete –
I retreated to the street in complete defeat.

My wife left the shop with a Cheshire Cat grin –
Her quest for the cigars was win, win, win,
Though not the cigars I came looking for –
Determined woman bought five – yes five – not four!

05-06-1996
Ft. Lauderdale, Florida
Mariotte Hotel & Marina

I have a good friend from Air Force Days that is a gifted artist and writer, and who knows what all else. He has written a Cook book with story line and recipes that were overwhelming and mind boggling. I told him I would try help to get it published. I then made an attempt that went nowhere. Thus the following poem was written as a means of introduction to the book.

Take a Chance

You really have to take a look –
At the recipes within this book,
These recipes by Sy Goff writ –
To demonstrate his taste and wit.

Each recipe that's here inside –
To someone out of history tied,
From Betsy Ross to Al Capone –
Their culinary prowess shown.

The recipes that here you find –
Are from a fertile, tasteful mind,
An artist with a touch of class –
Mixes recipes with stories crass.

Now with the recipes no guarantees,
That every appetite will please,
Bt their story line is worth a glance –
So on Sy's recipes – take a chance.

06-06-1996

More thoughts to Rotary Club I was a member of on the new leaders that would be managing the club.

Our Leaders

To members of this Rotary Club –
as your poet I've been named,
Now I want to make it very clear –
for that decision cannot be blamed.

No bard am I that would volunteer –
but the title I will respect,
And do my best to put into rhyme –
those subjects that "I" select.

My tenure begins on the first of July –
when Penny's our President,
She is one this decision did make –
a decision she soon may lament.

I start with thoughts in honor to her –
to thank her for taking the lead,
Like Royal and Wayne and Terry for sure –
she has what it takes to succeed.

Yes, Royal and Wayne and Terry are all –
leaders with skill and quite witty,
Penny has that with other traits strong –
such as classy and being more pretty.

Poem began this past year to praise –
then as always I let my mind wander,
So don't take offense at the sexist remark –
for I want not this moment to squander.

To Terry and Susie, Greg and Brad Seals –
accolades on their good works bestowing,
They are the engine gives Rotary its drive –
and direction where this club is going.

Let's raise a glass to the old and the new –
let all members here in good standing,
Toast to the past then pledge to support –
Penny Dear in her job – most demanding.

06-08-1996

Back to our Sunday School Faith Class. Gus Stewart gave a
wonderful Class lesson and asked if we would write something to
explain our belief in God. I wrote the following:

I believe

I believe in a God a Powerful Creator –
A Maker of all the Soul's liberator,
I believe in a God from which all things came –
I believe in a Power with God as name.

I believe in God as an unknown dimension –
I believe with death a new life ascension,
I believe when there I may have to atone –
For sins I've committed, my sins alone.

This God of Creation will not condemn me –
For sins of another I caused not to be,
This God has a purpose I someday will know –
And God in God's time this to me will show.

All my life actions when the body is done –
To be measured by God ere the next life begun,
I pray God's forgiveness for errors I've made –
Sins of omission when from good I have strayed.

This I believe knowing it may not conform –
With beliefs of another may not be the norm,
But here in this moment I feel God's release,
In the wonder of living this offers me peace.

Peace with the sorrows in life cannot change –
That life with God's Grace helped me rearrange,
This God of the Universe – deliverer of my Soul –
Is the God I believe in that makes my life whole.

06-09-1996

This next was written in Halletsville, Texas at the Bell Air
Restaurant to pass the time,   and yes – to fill an inner need.

Halletsville

I find that I have reached the age –
Where all in life is but a stage,
A stage where everything I see –
Is scripted for one person --- me.

The sights, the sounds, the things I feel –
To no one but my mind reveal,
These stage events are mine alone –
From my own vantage to be shown.

I sit and wonder at life's scheme –
And analyze as if in dream,
The many people here around –
To see what thoughts in them are found.

In Halletsville I have the time –
The stage of life to put to rhyme,
In a restaurant with the people there,
Who play their part the stage to share.

It's lunch time in this rural place –
And from a corner now I face,
A dining room with neat décor –
And pleasant folks not seen before.

A waitress dressed in blue jeans trim –
With friendly manner - proper, prim,
Does grace this place with country style –
As she takes your order with a smile.

A table see that is quite near –
Grandparents with grandchildren dear,
And well before their dinner done –
They brought to stage much love and fun.

A grand mix of diners come and go –
As across the stage of life they flow,
So quickly now the lunch time through –
In Bel Air Restaurant remain but few.

Back to the airport soon must go –
Where my passengers will never know,
The play of life was on my stage –
As they with their stage did engage.

Then from the runway we'll depart –
And on flight to Austin we will start,
New stage of life from heights on high –
As we bid this stage, Halletsville, goodbye.

06-18-1996

The city of Austin was going through the political trauma of
wanting to close their middle of the city airport to another
location. Bergstrom Air Force Base, located at the southern
edge of the city, was the focus. The flying community of which I
was a member was, for good reason, strongly opposed the move.
This next was the first of the poems I wrote to explain why. I
sent it to Kirby Perry who had generated a very large group of
"Save Mueller" supporters. It came to no avail and airport
movers won out. Robert Mueller airport is no more.

Robert Mueller

To me it's really very plain –
Robert Mueller Airport should remain,
No knowledgeable pilot can deny –
There is no better place to fly.

To Bergstrom there's no need to go –
For aircraft with noise level low,
These smaller aircraft have no need –
To that distant airport to proceed.

The Bergstrom airport that's far away –
For those noisier aircraft is "A" okay,
A downtown airport well designed –
With needs of the city can be aligned.

An aesthetic airport Austin could spark –
Beautify the city with a Business Park,
To me it's certain not matter of chance –
Attractiveness of city it would enhance.

No better location we ever could choose –
A valuable asset we never should lose,
So let's keep it here not throw it away –
As an airport Robert Mueller stay.

06-26-1996

I had a nephew who was a Chemist that was marrying another Chemist in San Francisco. We were going to join with other members of the family there to celebrate. We were flying into San Francisco and would pick up our Hertz Rental car for our stay there. But before the wedding we would be driving to Carmichael, California where we would be staying with my sister-in-law Mollie. On the Continental flight from Houston to San Francisco, to pass the time, I wrote the following with tongue in cheek. My sister-in-law has a lovely home that she keeps beautifully. We stay there fairly often.

Crass/Ingrate

On Continental Airlines we fly today –
From Austin across the U.S.A.,
To San Francisco we wend our way –
Where for David's wedding we will stay.

In a Hertz car rental we will drive –
From the Frisco Airport to Mollies dive,
At her home in Carmichael we will arrive –
And hope till the wedding will survive.

For the time we will be staying there –
Mollie offered us her house to share,
I'm sure that she did take great care –
The accommodations of her home prepare.

For before we came we both agree –
The sheets must fresh and spotless be,
Her home should from all dust be free –
Or she no happy guests will see.

From there to the wedding we will go –
To the Clarion Hotel in San Francisco,
To David's wedding where all will know –
What the state of Mollie's house did show.

With this poem we want clearly to state –
We don't mean it sweet Mollie to intimidate,
But her hosting had better be first rate –
Or we sure can be an ugly and crass ingrate.

06-30-1996
Continental Flight
From Houston (IAH) to San Francisco (SFO)

The following 10 poems were written in California.

Word Test

With Word I'm gonna run a test –
And try to do my very best,
To us the features there within –
So for that purpose I'll begin.

Just now it did so very well –
Word in my text to help me spell,
Very much to my delight –
Word dictionary spelled it right.

Another feature Word fulfills –
For me refines my typing skills,
Off the screen it helps me take –
These many typos that I make.

Words it helps me move around –
When better places for them found,
It's easy with the cut and paste –
So precious time I do not waste.

And when a different word I need –
With Word Wordfinder I proceed,
To pull up words there to peruse –
Then from the screen another choose.

This task I've set myself upon –
With Word I could on and on,
But surely I have said enough –
To show this program's really tough.

07-01-1996
Carmichael, Ca
Mollie's house

While at Mollie's, I had fun acclimating to her Apple Computer.
It was working fine, but having problems getting the data to
print on her printer. Thus the following.

Her Mac-in-tosh

I'm here at Mollie's with the time –
To put more silly thoughts to rhyme,
With Mollie's Mac-in-tosh I play –
To help me pass the time of day.

Now some who know not what I mean –
May think I'm being quite obscene,
That she would let me have my way –
Her Mac-in-tosh control and play.

But her Mac-in-tosh can't be abused –
It's a handy thing that's been well used,
When by my fingers skillfully stroked –
It's inner workings are provoked.

With creative fervor it then caught –
As it responds to all my thought,
I know to some may sound absurd –
It puts to rhyme my every word.

Yes her Mac-in-tosh is great to use –
A neat little thing that does amuse,
It's nice and with it I had fun –
But just can't finish the job begun.

The final climax it can't complete –
Won't give the desired outcome sweet,
In case you're wondering I'll give a hint –
Lacks the means to put it out --- IN PRINT.

07-01-1996

With thoughts of the wedding, and other ongoing events, I wrote
the following.   I did make a few needed changes to the original.

Chance

Miscellaneous thoughts in my mind ran –
That in marriage there is no perfect plan,
In life you have to take a chance –
For the fullness of it to enhance.

There's no such thing as a perfect mate –
Each person's different how they relate,
And no one knows when first they meet –
If that relationship will stay complete.

Sometimes it's hormones takes the lead –
Where harmony does of course succeed,
The relationship stays fast on track –
With warmth of feelings there's no slack.

But for a relationship to long endure –
The feelings must grow strong and pure,
There has to be a mutual give and take –
Where each one does for the others sake.

In a marriage there is no certainty –
That strong bonds will forever be,
There is no way for sure to know –
If a relationship with time will grow.

Each person though must do their best –
In a caring relationship love to invest,
To live their life with an ease of mind –
With the bonds of love in each they find.

If the relationship should fall apart –
Won't be the end must make new start,
There are wonderful people all around –
You may find another that's more sound.

Yes a relationship is a necessary game –
How on to this earth we all here came,
In the design of Creation for new life to live –
Live life to the fullest with the love you give.

07-01-1996
Mollie's house

Psychotic

My darling wife who is quite exotic –
Thinks I am sweet but at times psychotic,
And with her I cannot disagree –
Because at times I am you see.

It is poetry that makes me so –
Psychotic folks do that you know,
They organize within their mind –
In words to rhyme events they find.

Within my past in times of grief –
Was poetry that brought relief,
Events unclear I put to rhyme –
Were understood in measured time.

And I have found I do that still –
Poetry my needs fulfill,
There is no way to explain to you –
It is not a conscious thing I do.

So yes, psychotic I well may be –
But then would be a dichotomy,
Psychotic madness does explain –
And poetry ---- that keeps me sane.

07-03-1996
Mollie's house still

Damn Ram

Her Mac-in-tosh is now complete –
Can show a finished product sweet,
For a dandy printer we did find –
But the way we did it blows the mind.

One day we drove out all around –
At a trailer park a printer was found,
It just couldn't do the job we need –
So to many other places we proceed.

Now the trailer park had its own tale –
On all of our senses it did prevail,
It was a park less than first rate –
In fact it was in a deplorable state.

Within one trailer I found a mess –
The contents was in complete distress,
As well from a factory much too near –
Came a buzzing noise that hurt the ear.

From that park in haste we did depart –
As search for a printer again we start,
Then Mollie and Myrtle caused delay –
As we stopped for cherries on the way.

We found a place that had printers two –
And both it seems for her Mac would do,
With one the cost was much too high –
The other we thought not a very good buy.

Well Mollie knew of another good place –
And she drove us there at a rapid pace,
We bought a printer they had on hand –
At a price acceptable in an Apple brand.

Arriving home we then opened the box –
And we thought on us there must be a pox,
After reading the book I said "Oh damn"!
This printer won't work it needs more RAM!

Much too sophisticated was this one –
Our search for a printer still not done,
But we had enough for this one day –
Put it back in the box and out of the way.

That night at supper we heard from Anne –
And we made a change to acquisition plan,
At McClellan's Salvage and Surplus store –
She told us were printers and even more.

So next day to McClellan we drove in haste –
And sure enough there buried in the waste,
Hiding on a shelf and nearly out of sight –
Myrtle saw a printer that she knew was right.

Then another thing caught Myrtle's eye –
A tape recorder/player she just had to buy,
A teacher one like this had in her possession –
To purchase machine now became an obsession.

Though her logic I never fully understand –
We left with contraption and printer in hand,
She all my feeble pleas for sanity spurned –
So to primary needs of computer we returned.

We continued our search all around the town –
At computer store outlets of high renown,
For a cable and ribbon and paper we look –
That many more miles and more patience took.

Well finally home with the goodies in hand –
Hooked them all up and they looked so grand,
But printer still held us in utter contempt –
Refused to cooperate on the first attempt.

We won! We won!, we beat the darn thing –
That computer and printer together did sing,
Mollie is lucky cause till she gets more RAM –
With stats of her Mac I no longer give a DAMN!

07-03-1996
Yes, still at Mollie's

During our stay at Mollie's, I went shopping with the girls at a
local Supermarket. While in the Market, I couldn't help but
overhear two very loud speaking ladies expressing their views on
the next presidential election candidates. It was rather
humorous for they were oh so enamored with Bill Clinton and
were vocal about it. When we returned home I wrote the
following:

He Cares

I'm gonna vote for Clinton and Gore –
Though Clinton's morals I kinda deplore,
I will not vote for OLD Robert Dole –
That man is real mean and has no soul.

Bill with his charm makes very plain –
He really, really, really, feels my pain,
But Dole he lacks that vision thing –
Extremism and poverty I know he'd bring.

Now President Bill the Guv from Arkansas –
Has the best Command credentials you ever saw,
While Bob Dole that wimp from a Kansas farm –
Was a loser in battle fell and hurt his arm.

Ole Willie has so much suave and flair –
His bodily skills with Ms. Flowers did share,
While Bob that OLD Cad he left his first wife –
And put that hussy Elisabeth into life.

Our Bill is so poor cause he works for us –
Why is there with White Water such a fuss?
Bob and Elizabeth take more than their share,
That's how they became a rich millionaire.

And sweet little Hillary smarter than a man –
She got for us all a Universal Health Plan,
But that mean OLD Bob wanted another instead –
Wanted babies sick and those old folks dead.

And the FBI file with that scamp Livingstone –
Can't they leave poor Bill and Hillary alone,
It's clear he was hired with Bob's dirty tricks –
By those nasty Republicans just pure politics.

I love Bill Clinton and virtuous Hillary –
They both want to do so much for me,
While Dole and Gingerich, yes Limbaugh too –
All they want to do is give the shaft to you.

And all Bill's friends up there in Arkansas –
It's not his fault if they broke the law,
Bob Dole and all his cronies they did prevail –
It's they not them that should be put in jail.

Well I'm through with my sermon on the Mount –
And yes ethics and morals they somewhat count,
I know all about Bill's extramarital affairs –
But Clinton's my man because he cares – he cares~!

07-04-1996

This next, while still there in Carmichael at Mollies, I almost was
not going to include. But since I wrote it with humor, I did.

Crass and Gross

I find some jokes the Coats Clan tell –
May lead them to the depths of Hell,
I'm un-amused, at times appalled –
By jokes that have them all enthralled.

To tell their jokes takes lots of brass –
I find some really classless, crass,
These jokes from gutter probably came –
It seems they have no sense of shame.

I just don't think they really care –
When tasteless jokes with family share,
It's obvious to this bunch it's fun
When to gross sex their jokes do run.

But must admit this Clan is great –
That with such intimacy they relate,
I'm proud to be in this family close –
Even though their jokes are crass and gross.

07-05-1996

While there at Mollie's, my daughter Myrtle E. and her husband
Bob drove there from Seattle for the wedding. I usually have a
difficult time sitting through a movie. One night to pass the
time, my wife, Mollie, Myrtle E. and Bob watched on the
television the VCR movie Sabrina as I wrote this next.

Not For Me

To watch a movie is not for me –
I find it hard my thoughts to free,
I'm not very good with imagery –
So I can't relate to what I see.

No matter what, I analyze –
I can't sit back and fantasize,
Instead with logic I apprise –
The scenes presented to my eyes.

And when I do it's just not fun –
From time the movie is begun,
I try to think what I'd have done –
To life I live do my thoughts run.

So with most movies can't relate –
They're not for me a normal state,
The circumstances they create –
Unrealistic humor, love, war, hate.

Now with this poem I opine –
There are some may think it asinine,
That towards movies I do not incline –
And glad this problem not theirs but mine.

07-05-1996

Well we drove to San Francisco for the wedding to the Clarion
Hotel where other family members from around the country
would as well be staying. It was good seeing everyone and the
conversation flowed and flowed. Many stories were told by all
and I recorded one, I think humorously, that follows.

Meow

At the Clarion Hotel where we are at –
Jim told us a tale about his cat,
A Siamese much too old to keep –
They mercifully had to put to sleep.

Like Dr. Kevorkian they sadly began –
Use of Paregoric in a terminal plan,
This elixir to the cat they feed –
In hopes the plan would fast succeed.

With plan however they had a glitch –
For the cat developed a nasty twitch,
So gentility of plan they had to revise –
To send their kitty to its demise.

Jim put his hand over kitty's mouth –
With that of course the cat went south,
Went south into that far off place –
With Jim's gentle hand upon its face.

Jim's tale was done with kitty dead –
And then planted into a flower bed,
But if that task had been up to me –
A different passing kitty would see.

I would call Sam my brother-in-law –
The surest cat killer you ever saw,
Very little pain do his cats feel –
When run over by a heavy car wheel.

Then in a bag in the trunk of his car –
It is then entombed in a dumpster far,
Where Sam's friends who jog by it now –
In memory of kitty go Meow, Meow, Meow.

07-07-1996
San Francisco, Clarion Hotel

**This next was written after the marriage events and is the final
poem of this California series.**

Elixir

Two Chemists Lydia and Dave –
Decided marriage they would brave,
They for each other deeply cared –
So wedding vows this day they shared.

Before the wedding vows were made –
Joined chemicals to ply their trade,
A magic potion in a vial they mix –
For a lifelong bond it was a fix.

Fortune cookies then foretold –
What future had for them to hold,
And then those Chemists did recite –
Vows that they themselves did write.

The wedding one of grace and ease –
I know this union God did please,
Throughout the service I could feel –
The depth of love that each reveal.

With service done two lovers start –
New life together with one heart,
Their chemistry mixed a perfect blend –
To man and wife from just good friend.

07-07/08-1996
San Francisco
Kohl Mansion/Clarion Hotel

When back in Austin we fell into our normal routine again. I
was still with the Rotary Club and participating with wonderful
members in their activities. Some of the poetry I would write
that related to the Club would at times be published in their
Newsletter. This next is one of those as some of the others you
have read and are still to read that are in this collection

Installation

To Casa Caliche last Thursday we went,
Installation of officers again our intent,
At the invitation of Sue and Clift Price,
We shared an evening most pleasant and nice.

Drink and food for the evening was great,
As we with our past to our future relate,
In the Rotary tradition together we meet,
So Penny and others their pledge could complete.

Terry held court as the meeting began,
And followed as always an organized plan,
To all in position to make the club go,
He gave full recognition, his gratitude show.

His term now completed as president no more,
Came to the ranks where he was once before,
Clift did the honors Penny Dear to swear in,
Then she her new term as our president begin.

She told us her vision of what club could do,
And strength of that vision our energy renew,
We promised our president we would invest,
With her guidance and leadership our very best.

Proceedings soon over but before we depart,
A young lad with fiddle good music did start,
The talent he shared with us all gave a lift,
Complimented the evening – unexpected – a gift.

To Clift and Sue Price our hosts of the night,
The party near perfect, Casa Caliche just right,
Jerry G. said it best when he praised you as host,
So to you and this club let us all raise a toast.

July 11, 1996

I received a poetry book from my sister-in-law Mollie. This next was my response to her for being the wonderful lady I know her to be. The recent trip to her home, and then on to San Francisco for her son David's wedding, reinforced my thoughts and feelings towards her.

Dear Mollie

I thank you for your being –
for all you mean to me,
For your gentleness of spirit –
the good in you I see.

I thank you for your nature –
your caring steadfast way,
For warmth you give to others –
thoughtful things you say.

I thank you for your humor –
jokes you tell with flair,
Your expressions of enjoyment –
laughter that you share.

The fun you get from living –
even when the going is rough,
Gives testament to a lady –
very feminine but also tough.

So thank you for your blessings –
the poetry book from you,
And accept this verse as tribute –
you are a lady in all that you do.

07-17-1996
Thanks for a great time in your home!

This next is one that will always be remembered. A good Doctor Rotary member friend of mine lived by Lake Travis. He had a sailboat that he kept berthed at a marina by the lake. Having sailed the lake for many years, he knew it well, but the lake was substantially below normal due to a drought. One day seven of us went for a dinner sail. Thus this Oh Captain odyssey.

Oh Captain

Oh Captain, my Captain, our fearful trip is done –
We've past the rocky sandbar when the odyssey begun,
All dressed in white attire, your sailboat to enjoy –
I thought that shallow water, our outing would destroy.

Oh Captain, my Captain, to sail you first must float –
To get us off lake bottom you bravely left the boat,
Amid the rocks, the swell of wave, the perils of the lake –
So gallantly you did your best, the grip of bar to break.

Oh Captain, my Captain, though strong your efforts fail –
When Jerry joined to help you, ship still refused to sail,
While on the boat four ladies, so brave knew what to do –
Prepared to lighten up the load, get in the lake with you.

Oh Captain, my Captain, in my neat and white attire –
To join with you inside the lake, was far from my desire,
I used the ploy of telephone, to keep from getting wet –
But you persisted all ok, if the boat would lighter get.

Oh Captain, my Captain, I marched to orders clear –
I gave the ladies on the boat, all my possessions dear,
My cellular phone, my billfold, cash that need stay dry –
I joined with you in water, got soaked up past my thigh.

Oh Captain, my Captain, with your brilliance all agreed –
With ship afloat and day just right, on sail we did proceed,
Good to feel the blowing wind, from front and from the back –
How awed we were with your control, as with the wind you tack.

Oh Captain, my Captain, with you no need for fear –
Peg lost her hat and masterfully, lake waters you did steer,
You turned the boat and Jerry, for a moment had a choice –
As Peggy's hat he did retrieve, we all your skills rejoice.

Oh Captain, my Captain, when journey was nearly complete -
You sailed precisely to the dock, that hostile sandbar beat,
But came new challenge wind gusts strong, buffeted our ship –
And once again you took command, got us safely in the slip.

Oh Captain, my Captain, our triumphant adventure was great –
From the sail to scotch and water, to the chicken that we ate,
So tonight to the coffers of Rotary, my feet upon dry ground –
I give a buck in your honor, to the greatest Captain found.

Cheers to Captain Clift

08-05-1996

This next is one of my many inputs to our local newspaper
Letters to the Editor. I know they will not print them and send
them mainly to unload my thoughts on whatever it is that
inspired the need to write. Thus this next "Rock From Mars".

Rock From Mars

It came from space, from out the stars –
This fabulous specimen, rock from Mars,
It gave our scientists horrendous shock –
The primitive life form found in the rock.

Was such a remarkable thing that they saw –
Many conclusions from rock could they draw,
Religions bewildered, now God surely dead –
Creationism's tenets all stood on their head.

For 13,000 years that Mars rock from us hide –
Microbial life that was trapped there inside,
If found to be true what to us now is shown –
How dramatic! for surely, we are not alone.

Of tremendous advances, we're now on the brink –
But perish the thought, oh golly just think,
I just can't imagine, who could have thought –
God into this Universe, a new life form brought.

If dinosaurs remained, and their intellect evolved –
Would science and religion as ours be resolved,
If on finding this rock, this life? that we see –
Would dinosaurs pray, that a hoax it would be?

So many deep questions does Mars rock provoke –
As Mr. Writer, Sr. Editor from a city bespoke,
Would it be? Could it be? - he brilliantly coax –
My God Mr. Writer, is your commentary a HOAX?!?!?

08-10-1996

Once again this next is from a lesson given to our Sunday School
Faith Class by a wonderful teacher, a member of the class.

I Ain't

Like Gus sometimes I sit and ponder –
Just how I get to place up yonder,
And since I know I ain't no Saint –
I know too well I probably ain't.

That fact of life I have to face –
I'll probably go the other place,
That place the bible does foretell –
For sinners that is known as hell.

When I go there I'll surely see –
Some friends to keep me company,
Fire and brimstone will fill our day –
As for our sins we now must pay.

With this assessment I am not wrong –
I know good folks who there belong,
For since I know I ain't no Saint –
So too I know they also ain't.

Because of life that we are in –
Like me most people prone to sin,
And if they sin and don't repent –
They'll surely down with me be sent.

If Bible's prophecy observed –
Then Hell below for us reserved,
By us I mean those folks like me –
Who believe not Bible prophecy.

I know not what in Bible true –
So I won't be the judge of you,
But even if this partly so –
Predicts a crowd with me below.

As words of poem you try digest –
To make a point I write in jest,
To prove to you I ain't no Saint –
And also that a poet – I ain't.

08-11-1996

This next is another poem I wrote on our Rotary Club that I
Faxed to our Newsletter editor.

Review

Last week at Rotary we review –
With Howard Brunson what to do,
What we need do our Club to show –
And in so doing make it grow.

In Howard's words would not be tough –
If each of us just did our stuff,
We had to start that very night –
Walk out the door turn left and right.

Then all good people that we meet –
In fashion of this club now greet,
Express yourself and do it well –
As the goals of Rotary try to tell.

Relate things to our honored name –
Great University from which it came,
With sense of what is great and real –
To their best instincts now appeal.

Then if no one does heed our call –
We continue as a club that's small,
In cohesive strength let's realize –
What we achieve means more than size.

So to Howard a leader, wise, astute –
We raise a glass in respectful salute,
For founding this club and making it one –
We appreciate the hard work he has done.

08-14-1996

Another to the Rotary that was published in their Newsletter.

Stadium

Last week at the meeting our interest to peak –
On the status of stadium George Abikhaled speak,
Engineer of the project as it was re-designed –
With a look to the future of U.T. he aligned.

Now 73 million dollars is the estimated cost –
The logic for that on this audience was lost,
One member, facetiously, stated quite loud –
They wanted a campus for athletes to be proud.

Although that remark was said tongue –in- cheek –
It suggested a University with academics weak,
A school where football is the primary concern –
And a lesser objective is for students to learn.

Now that observation is to most quite unfair –
The highest of learning we know is found there,
It's just that a stadium is so visible to all –
The Arts and Sciences neath its shadow fall.

Athletics, yes football, is a strong guiding force –
The greatest attractions for a monetary resource,
Over 100,000 fans to watch football there throng –
Thus that edifice to income gives impetus strong.

08-16-1996

This next came with thoughts on something my Granddaughter
Halie generated. She had a school color assignment that she
wasn't happy about. I used this as a way to encourage her.

Color Assignment

The color blue brings to my mind –
So many different thoughts to find,
It makes me think of blue of sky –
And the blue seen in my mother's eye.

Now yellow brings another thought –
Happy times to me are brought,
So many nice things I find there –
Like the yellow in my sister's hair.

The color green brings to my eye –
A grassy field that I passed by,
So colors have a great affect –
On the many moods that I select.

This color assignment made me mad –
Terrible thoughts that my mind had,
It seems I tried too hard to do –
The task I thought required by you.

But everything is now OK –
With happy thoughts does my mind play,
Explaining colors now gives me delight –
With my mother's help it's now alright.

Granpa Tony

08-19-1996

Our Rotary Club participated in supporting the local Food Bank. Thus this that follows that was published in their Newsletter.

Food Bank

For last week's meeting we will thank –
Those members who went to the Bank,
The Food Bank Field Trip that they made –
Our respect to them is now displayed.

From those of us who couldn't go –
We want this special group to know,
That our best interests they support –
We look forward to their trip report.

Susie and Millie with Jerry went –
Where with other members they represent,
The Club's support for this community –
Their best foot forward for all to see.

We compliment those members all –
Who responded to the field trip call,
We're indebted for what they have done –
Our heartfelt thanks they've surely won.

They may be happy tonight to learn –
That more than accolades tonight they earn,
There's one of us who missed the trip –
Who will buy from the bar – them each - -- a nip.

Cheers!!!!

08-28-1996

This next again to Rotary. Don't remember if it was published
in the Newsletter for it is rather long.

None Better

Last week at our meeting, we had gala time –
So many things happened, to put into rhyme,
From a song to our Penny , that I had to sing –
To a talk on Genealogy, our speakers did bring.

Our President's birthday, the big FIVE "O" –
And she chose me to sing, Happy Birthday – solo,
With a look in her eyes, that was full of glee –
For that fund raising task, she put the onus on me.

Now to hear her song, from the voice she select –
Your vote with one dollar, she had to collect,
Was a unanimous vote, that you all did express –
For a Happy Birthday solo, 14 dollars said yes.

Then it was my turn, with bucks to decide –
Was it worth 15 dollars, your vote override,
I paid fifteen dollars, for I couldn't lose –
It was an honor for me, in whatever I choose.

Wanted Penny to know, that singing our choice –
To a wonderful woman, to raise up my voice,
From all of us there, in that meeting place –
Giving kudos to a lady, who leads us with grace.

This University Club, is more than just great –
In high Rotary traditions, we together relate,
From Jerry's singing event, we then quickly sped –
To Don's raffle offering, then numbers were read.

The numbers were read, and there was some delay –
For that winning ticket, which one of us pay,
For Don's Cream Liqueur, the drawing now done –
We assumed Mr. Lucky --- Wayne Hall surely won.

Millie gave me her glasses, my numbers to see –
And I couldn't believe it, the winner was me,
Liqueur and beer nuts, to table were brought –
I won the raffle, with those tickets I bought.

Yes I won the big prize, whoever would dream –
That was my lucky night, or so it did seem,
I was honored by Penny, birthday solo to sing –
And Don Wisthuff's liqueur, continued my string.

From there to awards, for attendance we went –
Recognizing those faithful, procedures intent,
Too many to mention, the cream from our ranks –
We gave them applause, as expression of thanks.

The meeting progressed, as the guests introduced –
An ex-Rotary President, and past Mayor produced,
She from Dripping Springs, he a leader from here –
Added much to the evening – when here they appear.

Then on to Ron's speaker, we all came to see –
Who would speak on our roots – our Genealogy,
He claimed was a novice, but he sure knew a lot –
How to seek out our history, was good info we got.

Two announcements were made, that I now must relate –
And they both are exciting, as a fund raising date,
Our own Dirk Van Allen, in his Golden Pond lead –
Bloody Mary's with Mark, as to the stadium proceed.

To Notre Dame vs Texas, courtesy of Mollie Lamphear –
Then bearded production, where shy Dirk will appear,
These thoughts of the evening, came quickly to mind –
So three cheers to this Rotary, none better to find.

08-30-1996

Well once again from the Church balcony -- follows ---

Who Me?

The sermon today is entitled "Who? Me?" –
Our minister will do the preaching,
His talk for sure will masterful be –
For Preacher is good with his teaching.

Our minister when his sermons prepare –
With the Spirit of God is imbued,
From Scripture lesson he's read with care –
Is the text of his lesson to continue.

"I Am who I Am", he has taken from text –
To impress what the sermon should say,
His thoughts wove together one to the next –
God is there, wants to show us the way.

The Burning Bush, God and Moses involved –
Thru the Bush God to Moses did speak,
Before the sermon was done and resolved –
Were told how God Moses did seek.

With guidance from God to Egypt went back –
The voice from the bush he obeying,
Led his people from bondage, Pharaohs attack –
His instructions from God not betraying.

The sermon enforced how Moses did heed –
The will of his God tried to follow,
Safe passage from Egypt with Moses succeed –
So "I Am who I Am" words not hollow.

Skillfully woven was subject "Who? Me?" –
It is "You" the sermon's professing,
"I Am who I Am" Bible wants you to see –
Is a God – all His people addressing.

09-01-1996

I have a very good friend who, in this electronic age, has given me the opportunity to purchase equipment he is not using. This next is on a computer printer in that category.

Much Better

I'm writing this poem Pat's printer to test –
To see if this Laser, Dot Matrix can best,
I have little doubt, for I'm sure that it will –
All my expectations from a printer fulfill.

Now this Laserjet hp is really quite nice –
Especially considering the very fair price,
Wasn't quite sure when I got it last night –
But cartridge replaced, it printed all right.

All right's a misnomer, as seen in this letter –
It is oh so much quieter, faster – much better,
Completed this task with an economy of time –
So better beware – you'll be flooded with rhyme.

There still are some things I would like to know –
Like how much memory is in the printer to show,
I know it's quite fast and I really like it a lot –
But how much damn RAM has this Laserjet got?

Well excuse me Jerry, for the verbiage I used –
Don't want your fine senses to at all be abused,
But with these few words I want to impress –
To pay for this printer – need Patrick's address.

Sincerely

09-05-1996

This next paragraph completed my thoughts on the poem that follows it, that I felt compelled to write.

Yesterday, sometime during the day, I heard somewhere the phrase "In the name of the Father". It moved me nearly to tears and has been on my mind since bringing back memories I have long since reconciled. The above is an effort to clear my mind of the emotion it triggered. I believe it succeeded

In His Name

In the name of the Father – is this prayer begun,
In the name of the Father – let His will be done.
In the name of the Father – oh help me to find,
In the name of the Father – contentment of mind.

In the name of the Father – oh give me relief,
In the name of the Father – console me in grief.
In the name of the Father – my soul open wide,
In the name of the Father – God heal me inside.

In the name of the Father – I need Your embrace,
In the name of the Father – Your solace and Grace.
In the name of the Father – my plea don't forsake,
In the name of the Father – this pain from me take.

In the name of the Father – I'm on bended knee,
In the name of the Father – In His Name – comfort me.

09-08-1996

Our Sunday School Faith Class generates many thoughts and feelings that at times I have to express in rhyme. What follows next is one of those times.

This Room

Within this room in Tarrytown –
this church in which we meet,
Faith Class members come each week –
our faith to make complete.

By many leaders we are led –
as religion we explore,
During fellowship of Sunday hour –
our faith renew, restore.

As membership of church has grown –
within these walls appear,
Children in a music group –
that meet when we leave here.

Then Thursday mornings women join –
within this room to stitch,
These quilters work with hands of love –
in an atmosphere most rich.

How different those activities –
now practiced in this place,
From Bible lessons, children's song –
to that of quilting pace.

Though not the same there is a bond-
when each endeavor is done,
The Faith Class, children, quilters all –
God's purpose join as one.

The sermon reinforced these thoughts –
of what room means to me,
That found within these hallowed walls –
are works can set Soul free.

09-15-1996

This next needs no explanation

Our Neighbor

Today we went across the street –
To our neighbor's home for a tasty treat,
She's a lady who is mighty neat –
A wonderful person hard to beat.

This neighbor is a high class dame –
Much classier than Aunty Mame,
She now adds cooking to her fame –
And Helen Skaaren is her name.

It was very much to our delight –
When my wife and I she did invite,
To share with her a tasty bite –
With food to please our appetite.

And so at noon with that intent –
To Helen's house today we went,
While there delightful hours were spent –
In repast that was pure content.

Talk was good, the wine was great –
Was really fine the food we ate,
Everything was just first rate –
As with our neighbor we relate.

So to Helen Skaaren thanks we send –
And these accolades to her extend,
The lunch she shared was special blend –
From a magnificent lady, "our neighbor" – our friend!

09-19-1996

The following is my critique of a Rotary meeting that I had
written and sent to the Editor of our Rotary News Letter.

Show

Tonight at Rotary what a show –
The entertainment was great,
Our speaker one that's in the know –
On the Rotary Foundation relate.

Before he spoke, the raffle prize –
By Susie Maloney express,
You give five bucks to view her size –
And then her weight you guess.

Now PHD Susie was mighty brave –
Her body to give to the game,
And Jerry Galbraith fifty bucks gave,
To one who the closest came.

Susie Maloney is neat and compact –
Her measurements in the right place,
Many dollars came in as eyes interact –
The curves of her body to trace.

The entries in, she stepped on the scale –
Looked at the numbers below,
Jerry's keen eye was one that prevail –
His guess won the prize of the show.

Rotary speaker Mike Pinson spoke –
Rotary Foundation his topic,
Depth of our giving in us he provoke –
And Jerry became philanthropic.

His fifty dollars and then fifty more –
He affably gave the Foundation,
Clift then continued as he's done before –
"Paul Harris Fellow" gave a relation.

As Penny with gavel put meeting to end –
Respect for our Rotary did grow,
All the events and what speaker extend –
Made me Rotary proud --- what a show!

09-19-1996

This next poem was sent to members of the Sunday School Faith
Class on my critique of a Class retreat many attended.

Fire & Stuff

Forrest had a burning desire –
To build for us a roaring fire,
So during the day he did collect –
Logs he thought were not too wet.

Then after dinner he did his part –
That big bonfire try to start,
With match and paper all he provoke –
Was not much fire but lots of smoke.

I joined him kindling wood to pick –
And I splintered up a walking stick,
That seemed to help a little bit –
But the wretched fire still gave a fit.

Then woodsman Herb he had a plan –
With some newspapers he made a fan,
Then the stubborn fire with it assailed –
But these laudable actions also failed.

Herb then attacked a cedar break –
Small branches from it he did take,
That green stuff into the logs he poke –
Results he got was lots more smoke.

Our Herb was not discouraged yet –
The kitchen drain board he did get,
With that we were a sight to see –
We fanners of the fire three.

We must have put on quite a show –
As flames in spurts did ebb and flow,
Then down to join came Gordon Ross –
Who took control and tried to boss.

That didn't set too well with me –
I have to be the boss you see,
Accepting this Gordon did his best –
And supported with his dry wit and jest.

I messed the fire up real good –
Thank goodness Jerry understood,
With kitchen drain board the fire fan –
It came to life -- boy what a man.

All this time the rest of our gang –
Abused us with their tawdry slang,
Their laughter made it very plain –
They really couldn't feel our pain.

Although our feelings they abuse –
Now blazing fire we let them use,
Marshmallows that on hangars prick –
Into "OUR FIRE" we let them stick.

Around that fire we then all sat –
To sing some songs and idly chat,
The songs it seems a repertoire –
Only was matched by the start of fire.

So many of their songs begun –
Not in right words before were done,
With that don't mean this bunch offend –
For all but one frog voce did blend.

Now as it must and as it will –
Came time the blazing fire to kill,
Because of the blister it gave to me –
With method I suggested not all agree.

We used the plan that others chose –
And Gordon directed the water hose,
While Myrtle in the middle did her part –
To help extinguish the fire we start.

That's the ballad of the Windsong fire –
If you ever need a fire starter to hire,
I suggest this Faith Class you avoid –
Of fire starting skills we're completely – devoid.

09-21-1996

The following 4 poems are related to a vacation my wife and I
took with close friends, the Galbraiths', to Italy. Our
granddaughter's school class in Houston, would send a stuffed
small bear with friends or family members who wanted to
participate in sharing their vacation using the stuffed bear as the
vehicle for relating their experiences. My wife agreed and we
took that little stuffed bear on our journey.

Not Wood

Oh Boy! - Oh Boy! - Hip hip hooray!!!
At last! – At last! – We are on our way!!!
We are on our way – what fun, what fun !!!
Our vacation to Italy has at last begun!

My name is Cruiser, and I'm a stuffed bear,
I am on a big airplane and going somewhere,
From a class room in Texas where journey began,
We are flying to Italy according to plan.

Halie's Grandma and Grandpa are going with me,
With their pals Peggy and Jerry here that you see,
In this picture at the airport in Austin they took,
I'm the one in the middle; come on – take a look.

Our first stop St. Louis which is on the way,
On our journey to Italy for fun and for play,
St. Louis to Washington to New York then to Rome,
We will all be exhausted before we get back home.

For friends in Spring Texas pictures we'll take,
Add to them some notes on the trip that we make,
So this picture in St. Louis, the one you now see,
That bear with the sandwich is Cruiser – that's me.

Well we're back in the sky I got off MiMi's lap,
I just don't understand it, she's taking a nap,
Why I'm oh so excited, how can she do that,
She should join my excitement – or at least sit and chat.

But as Cruiser the bear, I'm sure you all know,
With the pals of my school chums on fun trips I go,
So I'll let MiMi sleep and I'll try to be good,
For my heart's made of stuffing not out of hard wood.

In the Washington airport our stay will be short,
So there will be no pictures from there to report,
We stayed in the airplane and boy was I sore,
I was left by myself, neath the seat, on the floor.

We arrived in New York during dark part of day,
In a door in the terminal thought we doomed to stay,
But we escaped and on a ticket counter I was placed,
As our routing to Rome on our tickets was traced.

Then we got into this airplane and oh me oh my!
It was huge! so gigantic! didn't think it could fly!!!
I was wrong! We are soaring! this airplane is neat!
Wow! We're flying to Rome – and I'm in my own seat!

Cause I'm Cruiser a stuffed bear my eyes never close,
So I enjoyed the whole passage – I never need doze,
With the light of first morning when all were awake,
This picture of me, over France they did take.

Soon in Rome we'll be landing, an end this report,
To expressions in rhyme I'll no longer resort,
With the rest of my pictures just set your mind free,
Put your thoughts into writing as if you were me.

10-14/15-1996
Cruiser (As told to Tony)
TWA flights from Austin to Rome

Next is one of two poems written on TWA flights from Rome.

Interlude

The strains of music I now hear –
That flow so gently in my ear –
Does penetrate into my thought –
As with Vivaldi's music caught.

I hear the brass in trumpet sound –
The clash of symbols that rebound –
And as the concert through me flows –
Life's awesome beauty does disclose.

It puts in me emotion strong –
Immerses me in poet song –
A song of life with no compare –
I find within the music there.

As from Rome to Texas fly this day –
With all my senses does it play –
How strong, serene, the music heard –
Can't be explained by simple word.

Vivaldi now is not displayed –
A new composer is portrayed –
Sounds from a Master who knows well –
The feelings in his soul to tell.

From the strings of violins so sad –
Tchaikovsky andante cantabile had –
But on its close with warm delight –
Came sounds of trumpet – happy, bright.

But then the trumpets lost their joy –
In this next movement mood destroy –
From happiness to sorrow went –
The composers sadness there to vent.

Oppressive theme did not last long –
Concerto changed to happy, strong –
Symphonic score of a Master's choice –
That made the spirits again rejoice.

Vivaldi, Liszt, Tchaikovsky were three –
Whose symphonies now entertaining me –
God guide their hand when they did write –
The scores that open mind and sight.

As upon my life they now intrude –
I'm so grateful for this interlude –
I am thankful for this life I live –
Vision of heaven the music does give.

11-01-06

The second written on flights from Rome to Austin.

Share

Buon giorno, buon giorno, from Cruiser the bear –
This Italian greeting with school chums I share –
My stay there in Italy has gone by real fast –
With so many memories that will last and last.

I've sent you all cards from just every place –
So my travels in Italy with me you could trace –
The flying to Rome then the taxi and train –
Each card that I sent you my journey explain.

Their musical language I've picked up somehow –
When they say "See you later", Italians use "Ciao" –
There in the evening when they bid you goodnight –
Use the phrase "Buona sera", I think that is right.

What a fabulous journey, the good times we had –
Those wonderful Italians made me happy and glad –
Each day was an adventure, what fun, what fun –
From cab ride with Carlos until now the trip done.

I send you a card with my mark most each day –
From Rome then around Italy at the places we stay –
The roads much too narrow and the traffic was ugh!
The trains were so hectic with the bags that we lug.

From Sorrento to Positano, the mountains and sea –
Were really breathtaking, at times awesome to me –
By a ferry boat from Sorrento to Capri one day went –
And on that scenic island, two glorious nights spent.

From the port a Funucularri, that's a lift on a rail –
Took us up a steep mountain, we were glad didn't fail –
Rode it down the next day, then we boarded a boat –
And sailed out to Blue Grotto, that's a cavern of note.

We continued our journey as we left Capri soil –
Took a fast ship to Naples that was a jet Hydra-foil –
Then went on to Palermo in an ocean liner all night –
We slept in our small cabin and arrived at daylight.

Now Palermo is a city that we found not too clean –
We were all disappointed and you know what I mean –
But a four star hotel that we found there by golly –
Gave us all a good laugh for its name, it was "Jolly".

At Palermo we thought we would give nerves a rest –
A car rental from Hertz we were sure would be best –
So a maroon station wagon, a rental car there we got –
And though the driving was chaotic, we liked it a lot.

What joy, what elation, what freedom we found –
All the beauty of Sicily from the car did astound –
The vistas of mountains and old castles were great -
Then with paisanos in Realmonte with hugs we relate.

From Realmonte we drove the Mediterranean coast –
Spent one night near a castle with our Italian host –
We had a view from our window was hard to believe –
That we knew in the morning we would not want to leave.

But we left after breakfast through small towns did drive –
After a light lunch on Mount Etna in Taormina arrive –
Taormina is so magnificent built on a cliff in the sky –
With its beauty so astounding it can give you a high.

Because of our love for Taormina we added a day –
In this panoramic setting we had to lengthen our stay –
The views from our window, Mount Etna, the sea –
Was powerful, overwhelming, yet so peaceful to me.

Too soon from Taormina to Messina we had to go –
The narrow streets of the cities again we must know –
We drove out to the port and our car ferry we found –
Then we sailed to the mainland for Naples then bound.

The drive to Naples through Italy will never forget –
All the mountains, the tunnels, the fine people we met –
We found a tape of a good opera at a stop that we made –
And I sang loud to the sounds from the opera that played.

Then speaking Italian with a Sicilian dialect appeal –
At Hotel "Royale" in Naples we got us a good deal –
After check-in, our car, back to Hertz we turned in –
And our wrestling with baggage again did begin.

Two nights there in Naples, with bus tour to Pompei –
A tour most delightful, an Italian guide showed the way –
From the Royale in Naples, to the Triana in Rome –
That hotel, the Triana, lacked the comforts of home.

But we stayed at the Triana, in Rome two more nights –
And on the last we drove around to see the Rome lights –
Yes on that last night in Rome with a guide on tour bus –
Absorbed Rome – Bella Roma – that is now part of us.

So I'm here in my seat on this great big airplane –
And I'm doing my best with my thoughts to explain –
That this odyssey, this journey, this trip we just took –
I know all too well, would fill more than one book.

Now Halie, my dear, your good help is still needed –
Tell your friends the main reason my journey succeeded –
All those cards and the pictures, the stories I share –
Came with the help of your MiMi to Cruiser the bear.

Right now I'm so happy, although under duress –
So in another poem – there is something to confess –
I'll tell you who the culprit is that used Tripper's name –
But for now, cause I'm happy, I'll give grandpa – the blame.

11-01-1996
Cruiser (As told to Tony)
TWA flights from Rome to Austin

That 4th and last on Italy written in Austin

Mistake

Gosh, I sure hate to admit it, but I made a mistake –
When I used Tripper's name on the trip I just take –
I wanted to visit Rome on that great big airplane –
So when they called me Tripper, I didn't complain.

On our travels to Italy until back home we came –
They thought I was Tripper though Cruiser's my name –
But I just pretend, because I really wanted to go –
I waited until the trip over and then let them know.

To my class mates in Spring I hope you're not mad –
When I used Tripper's name I know it was bad –
But because I'm a stuffed bear and you like me a lot –
I sure hope you enjoyed all the cards that you got.
And Tripper, my good friend, I know he won't mind –
Cause like me he's a stuffed bear of the sturdiest kind –
A bear from Spring Texas who the world wants to see –
He would jump at the chance to travel big time like me.

When you look at the pictures, the travels we share –
Remember that it's Cruiser and not Tripper seen there –
But whether Tripper or Cruiser I want you to know –
I would use even your name , for a chance, just to go!

11-02-1996
Tony (Alias Cruiser)
Austin, Texas

Next is my introduction of my Rotary Club's Guest Speaker.

Guest

Tonight I introduce my guest –
Who time with us came to invest –
A man in life who has gone far –
A practitioner before the bar.

Now attorney friends I have a lot –
But he's the nearest one I've got –
Lives just down the street from me –
This lawyer's name is Jim Keahey.

With introduction please take note –
I brought tonight a book he wrote –
His columns in Lake Travis View –
Is bound to please and humor you.

So welcome please this swell guy Jim –
The prize tonight, his book, not him –
His "LAWtoons" writing is the best –
He's a terrific lawyer, my honored guest.

11-21-1996

This next is something that was again begun in church balcony
on Thanksgiving Sunday morning and completed at home.

Thanksgiving

I sit in church balcony a bible in hand –
As the service proceedings try to understand –
The Prayer of Confession pledge I now hear –
I can't seem to relate to, rings false in my ear.

To a Sovereign God the congregation does pray –
Prayer compares us to sheep who from flock go astray –
The words of the prayer by most members are read –
While I other thoughts in my mind pray instead.

With a pledge for new members to God being made –
For a better understanding of God I now prayed –
There then came a solo "Broken and Spilled Out" –
That held little meaning although it was devout.

Followed anthem on Thanksgiving with which I agree –
Praising God for all blessings around us we see –
Then from Matthew a lesson of goats and of sheep –
Reinforcing conclusions that NONE will God keep.

The sermon on that passage Preacher Silliman trace –
With his message attempted to put the bible in place –
Explaining the Scripture God's thinking portrayed –
And I with my thinking from his preaching now strayed.

The collection and blessings made the service complete –
Then with thoughts I collected left my balcony seat –
With confusion on God for God's understanding I pray –
As I walked down the stairs and got on with the day.

11-24-1996

More from church balcony, with minor change, on "Serenity"
thoughts during a Sunday School Faith Class discussion.

Serenity II

To live in peace with serenity –
Requires the mind to be set free,
Free from all the pain and strife –
That's found in every walk of life.

Within the sunlight we must dwell –
Evil thoughts from mind dispel,
Those that punish and confuse –
The mind must sort and quickly lose.

Must pick and choose so carefully –
Those things that bring serenity,
Morality, honor, love, faith, trust –
In harmony with mind adjust.

When in harmony with mind at peace –
All life's blessings will increase,
Our thoughts and actions now as one –
Serenity --- God's Will be done?

Serenity? --- as others cry?
serenity? --- their tears deny?
Their pain, the cause for them to weep –
Does serenity put mind to sleep?

It is state of mine – serenity –
And I know not all with me agree,
With other thoughts would they reveal –
Serenity – the peace they feel.

As on this earth we make our way –
In game of life in which we play,
We seek a peace, that heavenly place –
And will find it only in God's Grace.

There is no doubt through our own will –
With mind that God in us instill,
No peace on earth without God can be –
God's Grace holds the key – to – serenity!!

12-01-1996

It seems 100 years ago that the city of Austin seeking support for relocating the center of the city Municipal airport. This next is something I wrote and sent to our local paper's editor.

Robert Mueller

To me it is really very plain –
Robert Mueller as an airport should remain,
No knowledgeable pilot can deny –
Aircraft from there should continue to fly.

To Bergstrom the heavies all should go –
But those aircraft with noise level low,
These smaller aircraft have no need –
To the Bergstrom airport to proceed.

For the neighborhood to have fair play –
Then the Bergstrom airport is "A" OK,
But the State and City should be aligned –
With a downtown airport that's well designed.

A clean environment good planning could spark –
Compliment the city with a business park,
To me it is certain not matter of chance –
The Austin economy it would surly enhance.

This valuable asset we never should lose –
So keep Mueller open is the option to choose,
Let's keep it here and not give it away –
As an airport for Austin – Mueller must stay.

12-08-1996

With my son-in-law Gary, we took the grandchildren to a local play area, Discover Zone. While there and the children were happily playing, found myself in a melancholy mood and wrote -

Illusion
(To the music of Evita)

I look at life that here surrounds me now –
I'm overwhelmed,

By emotions that I feel down deep inside me –

All this confusion –
Are all the sights, the sounds, the depths my senses feel –
Are they illusions to me?

And as I try to make some sense from it –
The love inside,

For the children that into my life have wandered –

They are the future –
They are the reason that gives life its energy –
So real and precious to me -----

They take away all my confusion –
I know they can't be illusion –
They're much too real – their love I feel –
They are the promise ---- give life its purpose.

Now as these thoughts continue through my mind –
The hurt and pain,

From a past I've tried so hard to put behind me –
Past I have buried –
Within a heart round which a barrier wall I've built –

A wall containing my tears.

And as these memories through the wall now seep –

I look around –
To draw comfort from the atmosphere surrounding –

I seek forgiveness –
And understanding for mistakes that I have made –
These children give that to me.

Their innocence strengthens and holds me –
they free me from my confusion,
They are my hope – they are my joy -----
they are forever ----- and not illusion!

12-14-1996

This next was begun in our Sunday School Faith Class room
prior to members arriving. It was continued in the balcony
during church service and completed at home later in the week.

Religion

As in this room I sit alone –
I find religion overblown,
Upon Creation my thoughts dwell –
Religion's meanings – heaven, hell.

There is no doubt while I am here –
In this dimension's atmosphere,
Those elements my life embrace –
I have to try to keep in place.

It's certainly religion's goal –
To give the body meaning --- soul,
That all to a Higher Power belong –
It gives to each a focus strong.

A focus offering but one choice –
An Eternal God to praise, rejoice,
To help our life to rearrange –
For the next dimension's needed change.

Religion thus tries to ignite –
In this dimension a Holy Light,
A Light where purpose of life is found –
An Eternal God that's all around.

Of the many religions that I see –
I can easily accept Christianity,
The God of love it does extend –
God of forgiveness --- God of pretend.

Love and forgiveness go hand in hand –
A message for living I understand,
In the realities of life this message shown –
That's why religion, to me, overblown.

There is a purpose for all this to be –
A reason I'm here in this person called me,
Yes there's a Power all this Create –
And Religion – which one? – how do we – relate?

12-19-1996

This next was to my wife for our 40th anniversary.

Forty

For forty years she's led the pack –
This lady who does scratch my back,
She's been in front of all the rest –
Without a doubt she is the best.

She was beautiful when first we met –
And thus three children we beget,
Three daughters who I know for sure –
Are like their mother, sweet and pure.

Yes forty years that is a lot –
This life with her that I begot,
Beget, begot – helps me describe –
Beginnings of Coats/Melli tribe.

Now in last sentence you will see –
That Coats does lead the Melli tree,
My daughters like their mother look –
They're lucky Coats genes in them took.

And in grandchildren there's no doubt –
Their MiMi traits hold lots of clout,
I look at them and see her there –
Their face, their eyes. the love they share.

At this time of year I can never find –
A card that tells what's on my mind,
There isn't one that can reveal –
Her beauty, goodness, sex appeal.

Now a ruby is token befitting this day –
So with poem and rubies I want to say,
The very best years I've had in life –
Are those that I shared with my best friend – my wife!

Happy Anniversary with all my LOVE

12-21-1996

This next is my response to a poem I received from a close, dear
friend who was advanced in age. She had lost two husbands and
seeking my opinion on her relationship with an elderly Doctor
who had lost his wife. It was a moving poem with the theme
being, if heaven gave a second chance. My response that I gave
to her and him I titled, "Second Chance".

Second Chance

If heaven gave a second chance –
If there should be that circumstance,
Would we youth's passion want restore?
Or something deeper in our core?

As we give life a backward glance –
What from the past would we enhance?
From heaven what would we implore?
What in this life do we deplore?

If for a moment we could change –
Our mind and body rearrange,
With all the heat of younger age –
Would we with ardor now engage?

Once we have turned emotion free –
Would youthful passion heaven be?
Is heaven found in loves embrace?
Or in the soul – the now to face?

Here in the present we belong –
Sharing a love that binds us strong,
Not of youth's passion, far more whole –
A love of mind, and Spirit, Soul.

Now having both would be quite nice –
But either one would sure suffice,
Since I have you and you have me –
What else could heaven – really be?

12-29-1996

This Third Book

This is the last thought in my third book,
And to those who took the time to look,
I hope you found the reading worthwhile,
With my imperfections and writing style.

Since a professional poet I claim not to be,
I know many errors in my book you did see,
My thoughts on page was book's main intent,
For more as a diary is this book really meant.

08-30-2010

Poetry progression by Title and date:

Empty Nest -------------------------------- 01-07-1993
Class --------------------------------------- 01-02-1993
Inauguration ----------------------------- 01-20-1993
Ross Perot -------------------------------- 01-22-1993
Acapulco Odyssey, I ------------------ 02-01/02-1993
Doctrine ---------------------------- 02-02/07/08-1993
Acapulco Odyssey, II --------------------- 02-08-1993
Acapulco ----------------------------------- 02-09-1993
Acapulco, III ----------------------------- 02-09-1993
Ego ------------------------------------- 02-15/16-1993
Dear Ross --------------------------------- 03-02-1993
Black/White ------------------------------- 03-06-1993
Journey To Forever ---------------------- 03-13-1993
Dreams ------------------------------- 03-22/23-1993
Change ------------------------------------- 04-02-1993
Who I Am ---------------------------------- 04-03-1993
Because I Love You ---------------------- 04-09-1993
Pilot Time --------------------------------- 04-10-1993
Rotary ------------------------------------- 05-06-1993
Resignation ------------------------------- 08-04-1993
Clan --------------------------------------- 08-11-1993
Phantom ----------------------------------- 08-22-1993

Amazing Grace ---------------------------------- 06-06-1994
Unchanging ------------------------------------- 06-08-1994
Logic --- 07-03-1994
As One -- 07-09-1994
They Came -------------------------------------- 07-09-1994
Healing ------------------------------------- 08-20/21-1994
Family -- 08-30-1994
Plan --- 09-??-1994
Liz --- 10-23-1994
Rest --- 10-31-1994
Hero -- 11-12-1994
Out of Touch ----------------------------------- 11-16-1994
The Dinosaur ----------------------------------- 11-18-1994
Leaps & Bounds -------------------------------- 11-26-1994
Elvis -- 12-07-1994
Teach --- 12-11-1994
Potter --- 12-14-1994
Rotary Toast ----------------------------------- 12-16-1994
Ice Not Nice ------------------------------------ 12-19-1994
Leo Plan -- 12-31-1994
Ambience --------------------------------------- 01-05-1995
Mother's Love ------------------------------ 01-06/07-1995
Rigolleto --------------------------------------- 01-12-1995
Loyalty --- 01-22-1995
I Learn --- 01-22-1995
I Give --- 01-22-1995
Priority --- 01-24-1995
Valentine --------------------------------------- 02-02-1995
Again --- 02-09-1995
If I Could Sing To You -------------------- 03-04/05-1995
Long Shot --------------------------------- 03-17/18-1995
Key --- 03-24-1995
Seattle -- 03-29-1995
To Be Or Not To Be --------------------------- 03-31-1995
Oaklawn -- 04-01-1995
Respect --- 04-01-1995
Our Song --------------------------------------- 04-02-1995
What Was That ??? ---------------------------- 04-05-1995
Hot Tip --- 04-14-1995

Grady's Grill ------------------------------------- 04-15-1995
Embrace --- 04-20/21-1995
Wine -- 04-21-1995
Branson Report ---------------------------------- 04-27-1995
Discovery Zone ---------------------------------- 05-13-1995
Myrtle E -- 05-26-1995
Master Plan ------------------------------------- 05-27-1995
Quail --- 05-28-1995
Blessed --- 06-04-1995
Hold Dear --------------------------------------- 06-10-1995
Fine Wine --------------------------------------- 06-13-1995
Fiftieth --- 06-20-1995
I Love America Because -------------------------- 06-21-1995
Celebrate --------------------------------------- 06-23-1995
Presence -- 06-23-1995
Friend -- 06-29-1995
Fishing --- 07-01-1995
Divine -- 07-02-1995
Myths --- 07-09-1995
Inverter --- 07-12-1995
Family Fun -------------------------------------- 07-23-1995
Flavor -- 08-01/02-1995
Not Poetry -------------------------------------- 08-03-1995
P.S. -- 08-04-1995
Casa Caliche ------------------------------------ 08-08-1995
More Wine -------------------------------------- 08-25/26/27-1995
Exhilerama -------------------------------------- 09-03-1995
Bad, Bad, Bad ----------------------------------- 09-03-1995
Intact --- 09-17-1995
Last Report ------------------------------------- 09-23-1995
Complete -- 09-23-1995
Energy -- 09-24-1995
Luke 12:13-21 ----------------------------------- 10-01-1995
OJ --- 10-03-1995
The Ballad of OJ -------------------------------- 10-03/05-1995
Blind --- 10-08-1995
Oughter --- 10-12-1995
Slurp & Burp ------------------------------------ 10-12-1995
Puke -- 10-17-1995